1	丶丶ノ丬	十火			
2	氵汇汇	汇汇汇			
3	汇				
4	亻们们	佰佰佰佰			
5	佰				
6	フ丿丨彳	十土	37	亠	言亡去文亦立
7	犭子弓巾山幺	女工王	38	宀它室	
8	扌		39	艹	
9	木		40	十土士	圭耂卜止共山
10	禾米耒	礻衤方牛矢	41	夂大夫类木	羽竹隹雨
11	糸		42	口日目中	田四西
12	口日	田目貝	43	other ▯	
13	歹石酉	足虫車卓耳牙	44	丶ノ丷	八
14	言		45	儿几廾匕	十寸巾
15	月舟	阝艮良	46	小示水糸	刀力木
16	金食	区馬篭魚	47	丷业川小	心
17	other ◧	…	48	一	山土止
18		…	49	乂又夂女	止火大工王
19	丶丶ノ彡	匕卜卜乚匕匕	50	丁干子手	厶云仒衣匚
20	丨刂少	工丁亍干平	51	口	
21	十土士生朱失	弋戈戋	52	曰白月	田由母屯里車
22	斗才寸犬	巾甫隹主羊	53	目且貝見	石皿皿虫言
23	力刀勹	立文交亢方	54	other ◧	
24	欠夂	又反皮及	55	厂厂ナ右	广疒虍
25	己包也屯	几斤死	56	尸戸耂	other ◳
26	口田由申甲	白且見頁	57	辶	
27	卩阝尺月	殳艮良司	58	夂走	other ◱
28	厶区乍長	虫鳥鬼	59	…	
29	殳支圣卆	分令佥青寺	60		
30	合台谷各舌	召兑	61		
31	other ◨	…	62	…	
32		…	63		
			64		

MW00749410

KANJI
Fast Finder

Laurence Matthews

TUTTLE PUBLISHING
Boston • Rutland, Vermont • Tokyo

To Alison – for everything

Published by Tuttle Publishing, an imprint of Periplus Editions (HK) Ltd,
with editorial offices at 153 Milk Street, Boston, MA 02109 and
130 Joo Seng Road #06-01/03 Singapore 368357

LCC Card No.: 2003110210
ISBN: 0-8048-3393-1
ISBN: 4-8053-0720-X (for sale in Japan only)

Printed in Singapore

Distributed by:

Asia-Pacific
Berkeley Books Pte Ltd
130 Joo Seng Road, 06-01/03
Singapore 368357
Tel: (65) 6280 1330
Fax: (65) 6280 6290
Email: inquiries@periplus.com.sg

North America, Latin America & Europe
Tuttle Publishing
364 Innovation Drive
North Clarendon, VT 05759-9436, USA
Tel: (802) 773 8930
Fax: (802) 773 6993
Email: info@tuttlepublishing.com
www.tuttlepublishing.com

Japan
Tuttle Publishing
Yaekari Bldg., 3F
5-4-12 Osaki, Shinagawa-ku
Tokyo 141-0032, Japan
Tel: (03) 5437 0171
Fax: (03) 5437 0755
Email: tuttle-sales@gol.com

Indonesia
PT Java Books Indonesia
Jl. Kelapa Gading Kirana
Blok A14 No. 17
Jakarta 14240, Indonesia
Tel: (62-21) 451 5351
Fax: (62-21) 453 4987
Email: cs@javabooks.co.id

08 07 06 05 04
8 7 6 5 4 3 2 1

INTRODUCTION

Kanji (Japanese characters) are fascinating, but can be frustrating. In particular, looking up kanji in a traditional dictionary can be a nightmare as there is no "alphabetical order."

With this book you can find a kanji in seconds from its appearance alone. From the finder chart inside the front cover, you can turn to the correct page immediately, and finding the kanji on that page has also been made as simple as possible. As an optional feature you can make a double thumbnail index (see page xiii) to speed things up even more.

The Fast Finder is designed primarily for serious learners of kanji and serves as a quick reference for experts, but it is also suitable for beginners, or people who wish to dip into kanji, browse, or simply discover what a street sign means.

With this book you can:

- Find kanji quickly, reliably and intuitively—from their visual appearance alone;
- Quickly check the meanings, readings, stroke-counts and radicals of kanji;
- Look up newly encountered kanji or check ones you have temporarily forgotten;
- Track down elusive kanji more easily than in large kanji dictionaries;
- Simply browse and explore, comparing similar kanji.

There are some hints on finding kanji on page vii, but the system is so intuitive that you can try it right now: for example, try finding 独 or 空 . By the time you have looked up half a dozen kanji, you will appreciate the speed with which you can locate kanji in the Fast Finder.

I wish you success, fun and enjoyment in your study of kanji. Ganbatte kudasai!

Kanji

Although many thousands of kanji exist, the Japanese Ministry of Education has designated an official set of 1,945 *jōyō* (general use) kanji. You will see other characters around, particularly those used for names, but these *jōyō* kanji, together with numbers, punctuation and the *hiragana* and *katakana* alphabets (see inside the back cover), essentially constitute the everyday modern Japanese writing system. This book contains all the *jōyō* kanji.

Traditional dictionaries use a system of kanji components called "radicals" to classify kanji. Unfortunately, this system has many pitfalls for the beginner (and even for native speakers of the language!). Thus most dictionaries and kanji guides have indexes ordering the kanji by stroke-count (number of pen-strokes needed to write the kanji) and by reading (pronunciation). However a stroke-count index is slow and unpredictable to use, and a reading index is no help if you don't already know the reading of the kanji. Various systems have been devised to help with this problem: all of them associate codes (such as 2f6.4 or 1-4-2 or 3.1/3) with kanji—and most such systems depend on stroke-counting. This book arose out of my own frustration with these methods when learning kanji, and uses instead the human brain's pattern-recognition abilities directly.

The radical system is basically a good one, but not as logical as one might hope, and experts tend to forget how difficult it was to master the radical system initially. The Fast Finder uses "intuitive radicals:" kanji components which you think *ought* to be radicals are treated as such. Most symbols in the finder chart *are* forms of the traditional radicals, though, and so as you use the Fast Finder you will become more familiar with radicals and their quirks, and this will smooth your way to using the many books and dictionaries which are based on the traditional radicals.

Information given

The purpose of this book is to *find* kanji quickly, and to this end the amount of clutter on each page has been kept to a minimum. Thus the information given for each kanji is basic. However, the information is sufficient to determine the meaning of a kanji, to check at a glance any kanji you have confused or temporarily forgotten, or to look up the kanji quickly in your favorite dictionary or kanji guide for fuller information.

Below each kanji are five lines of information. The first two lines give the basic meaning(s) of the kanji and are meant to be read together; if only one line is needed then the second line simply has the symbol "–" For more on meanings, see page x.

The third line gives the kanji's *on* reading (Chinese-derived pronunciation) in capital letters, and the fourth line gives the kanji's *kun* reading (native Japanese pronunciation) in lower case letters. Readings are separated by spaces if the kanji has more than one. All officially approved readings are given. The symbol "#" means that the kanji has no (approved) *on* (or *kun*) reading, and "–" indicates a prefix or suffix. For more on readings, especially the notation used for *kun* readings, see page xi.

The last line of information for each kanji gives its "official" radical and stroke-count. Radicals are listed in Table 1 at the back of the book. In most cases the radical given is the traditional radical, but in a few cases, for historical reasons, the traditional radical is misleading or confusing, and dictionaries differ in their views about which radical to use instead. In these cases an asterisk "*" follows the radical number. The radical listed is that used in the ***New Nelson Kanji Dictionary***, and the traditional radical and alternatives are given in Table 2 inside the back cover.

The stroke-count of the kanji will help you to look up the kanji in the stroke-count index of a large dictionary (although using a reading index is easier, if there is one), and will also be of use if you are using a dictionary based on stroke-count of kanji components. The stroke-count for most kanji is universally agreed, but unfortunately in a (very) few cases dictionaries will disagree on stroke-count too.

Hints on finding kanji

It is a good idea to look through the book to get a feel for how the kanji are organised and displayed. The Fast Finder is organised with many kanji to a page, so that you can see at a glance the kanji which share a particular radical – and you can profitably browse this way too.

Dividing up a kanji

Initially you might find you have a tendency to regard any kanji which doesn't split left-right as indivisible; but you will see that the kanji on pages 62-64 (the "indivisible" kanji) are generally quite simple ones. The vast majority of kanji *do* divide into components.

To find a specific kanji, first look at how it naturally breaks down into components. Having split the kanji, choose the simpler component as your radical, which you will use to look up the kanji. If the components look roughly equal in simplicity, choose either; if you already recognise one of the components as a radical, you can use that. The same kanji may be found in two places: for example you will find 引 under ▌ on page 7, and also under ▐ on page 20.

In fact many kanji are to be found in several different locations in the Fast Finder. A consequence of having compact information for each kanji is that the whole entry can be repeated in each of these locations, thus eliminating the need for cross-references, and avoiding any need to decide which radical is "correct."

Although most kanji split left-right or top-bottom, don't forget the other patterns (pages 55-61). For these kanji, use the enclosing component as the radical.

Sometimes there is a choice of how much of the kanji to take as the radical. For example, when looking for 畑 , is the radical 丿 or 火 ? In most such cases, both radicals will be on the same page to make it easier to find the kanji (in odd cases where they are not, then the kanji will be found in both places). Kanji with several reasonable lookup methods are listed under all of these. But I rely on you not to make "unnatural" divisions: 聖 is in the ▬ section under 王 , not 土 .

Finally, if looking for a kanji which also serves as a radical, treat it as a kanji in its own right. For example, you would look up 鐘 under █ on page 16, but 金 itself under ▬ on page 34.

Finding the right page

Look for your radical in the finder chart inside the front cover. Remember to look in the correct section of the finder chart (█ or █ , etc.) as several radicals appear in more than one section. The arrangement of the radicals in the finder chart is intuitive, with similar radicals grouped together, and the simpler ones generally coming before the complex ones. If you can't find the radical in the finder chart, look on the relevant "others" page (these are pages such as 17, 18 and 43, and contain the radicals which have only one or two kanji each). You will very quickly become familiar with the common radicals, which appear explicitly in the finder chart, and hence sense when to look on the "others" pages.

As illustrated on the inside front cover, if a radical has many kanji then they will be subdivided according to how the remainder of the kanji divides up. In the case of two particularly common radicals which flow onto two pages (pages 2-3 and 4-5), this idea is used in the finder chart too.

For "indivisible" kanji, the shape of the top of the kanji is used; you can see how this works by glancing through pages 62-64. The same idea is used for the "others" pages and implicitly elsewhere.

Finding the kanji on the page

When you turn to the correct page, check at the top of the page that your chosen radical is there. (The thin vertical gray lines in the finder chart inside the front cover indicate whether to look on the left hand or right hand page).

The kanji for the same radical are grouped together: again, the arrangement is intuitive with the simpler kanji coming before the more complex. Kanji which are very similar and likely to be confused, such as 何 and 伺 , or 殻 and 穀 are placed close together. As above, if a radical has many kanji then they will be arranged according to how the remainder of the kanji divides up.

If the kanji itself is printed in gray, then you were not really looking for it in the right place: never mind, at least you have found it! However, the same kanji will appear elsewhere in the book, printed in black. As you use the Fast Finder, taking a closer look at these gray kanji will help you to appreciate more precisely how kanji components fit together and to distinguish between similar and easily-confused components. You are bound to find some gray kanji where you would not imagine that anyone would look for them, but rest assured that there are people who would, and did!

Important distinctions

If you are new to kanji, then there are several variants to watch for. Make sure you distinguish between radicals such as ⼀ and ⺍ , or 刂 and 刀 , for example. You will learn these distinctions with time (in fact, pretty quickly).

On the other hand, unfortunately, some variants denote the same kanji. A few kanji have minor variations from one typeface to another, or are slightly different when hand-written, and some slightly older versions of kanji components are still around. Space precludes listing all these variants. For example,

令 is the same as 令 and 曷 is the same as 曷 .

Kanji also incorporate relics from much earlier times. For example, many traditional radicals have several forms, depending on whether they appear to the left, right, top, bottom, etc. of the kanji to which they contribute (see Table 1 at the back of the book). Thus:

犭 and 犬 are different forms of the "dog" radical;

忄 and 心 are different forms of the "heart" radical.

To further complicate matters, many of these forms have different stroke-counts, which means that in some dictionaries finding even the radicals is a problem! In the Fast Finder all of these forms are treated as though they are different radicals, in the general belief that although facts about the kanji and their historical derivations can be fascinating, they should not frustrate your attempts simply to *find* a kanji.

Meanings

The English meanings given are as short and concise as possible; their purpose is to "suggest and remind" as one book puts it. From the meanings given, you will usually be able to deduce the meaning of the kanji in a given context, but note the following points.

Kanji do not usually correspond neatly to single English words. Like an English word, a kanji may have several distinct meanings. (If so, do not assume that the meanings correspond in any one-to-one manner with the readings. A kanji dictionary will make it clear which readings can take which meanings).

Where several meanings are given, similar meanings are separated by commas and distinct meanings by semicolons. If two meanings are separated by commas then they may qualify each other: thus "firm, hard" indicates firm to the touch rather than either industrial organisation or difficult. A particular phrase to note is "state, condition" which is used for a number of kanji meaning state, condition, situation, circumstances (as opposed to provide verbally, nation or proviso). Sometimes a kanji has a huge range of meanings depending on context, and this is indicated by "…"

Conversely, several kanji may share a common English meaning, so be wary of using this book to translate in the English-to-Japanese direction (another issue in this context is honorifics: words such as "give" and "receive" often have connotations of humility or conversely "deigning to" attached to them, which are generally not indicated in the Fast Finder).

Current rather than original meanings are given. The kanji 十 historically meant "needle" but now usually means "ten", so the meaning "needle" is not given.

Meanings given in italics (e.g. *tatami, haiku*) are Japanese words: any you don't recognise will often be obsolete units of weights and measures, such as *monme, rin, shaku*.

Transitive and intransitive verbs, and indeed nouns, verbs, and adjectives, can often be converted easily into each other in Japanese by adding different endings to the kanji, which acts like a "stem" in English. For example the kanji 憎 , "hate," is used for:

niku*mu*	to hate
niku*i*, niku*rashii*	hateful
niku*shimi*	hatred

where the portions written in italics are grammatical endings spelled out with *hiragana*. (See inside the back cover—and note that many books use parentheses instead of italics, writing niku(mu), etc.) The meaning of the kanji may be given as the noun, the verb, or the adjective: whichever is simplest, clearest, and least ambiguous.

Finally, "counters" are omitted from the meanings listed. Quite a few kanji serve as counting units for nouns, analogous to the word "head" in "six head of cattle." Counters are usually easily recognised in Japanese as they always directly follow numbers.

As far as compounds (words made up of two or more kanji) are concerned, their meanings can be guessed, more often than not, from the context and the meanings of the individual kanji. But of course many derived meanings are somewhat oblique, in the same way that English words such as "laptop" and "honeymoon" have meanings not implicit in their component parts.

Readings

Kanji have two sorts of pronunciations or readings: *on* and *kun* readings. Most kanji have one of each, but many kanji have several; and many others have an *on* reading but no *kun* reading or vice versa.

On readings are derived from Chinese; by and large they are used in compound words consisting of two or more kanji taken together. *Kun* readings are the native Japanese pronunciations of words; they are generally used for kanji which stand alone or with *okurigana* (grammatical endings spelled out in *hiragana*). Thus 車 meaning "vehicle" is pronounced *kuruma* when on its own, but it is pronounced *sha* in a compound like 電 車 *densha* which means "train, streetcar." This means that when you are looking for a compound word in an alphabetically-arranged Japanese dictionary, you will tend to be using *on* readings.

All officially approved *on* and *kun* readings are given. However, for clarity and to save space, the full list of possible *okurigana* for each *kun* reading is not given. *Okurigana* are given in italics; the symbol ".." shows that the reading may take other *okurigana* as well. If there are several *kun* readings, *okurigana* for subsequent ones are simply indicated by the symbol "+"

Thus the listing for *niku* (see the previous page) is rendered simply as niku*mu*.. In a similar way:

hay*ai*, hay*amaru*, hay*ameru*	becomes	hay*ai*..
ashi, t*aru*, t*ariru*, t*asu*	becomes	*ashi*, t*a*+

Providing a kanji has a *kun* reading, the fastest way to locate the kanji in a large kanji dictionary is usually to look up this *kun* reading in the reading index, and for this reason the Fast Finder always provides at least one set of *okurigana* (unless the kanji has a *kun* reading without *okurigana*, like *ashi* above, in which case use that).

Readings sometimes undergo minor changes in compounds (e.g. –*kane* might change to –*gane*), and there are also irregular readings for some compounds. The Fast Finder does not list these variants and irregular readings.

Thumbnail index

A unique feature of the Fast Finder is the option to make a double thumbnail index, as illustrated in the diagram below. This speeds up the use of the Fast Finder even more. This is especially noticeable if you are using it repeatedly to look up many kanji.

The thumbnail index allows immediate access to any page directly from the finder chart inside the front cover. Simply find the desired radical in the finder chart as normal, then put your right thumb on the tab with the chosen page number to open the book at the correct page. This tab will be on the same horizontal line as the radical you have found (so this actually bypasses the need to note the page number).

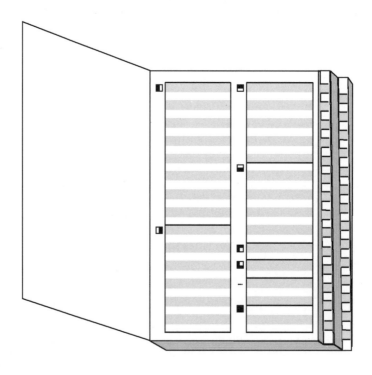

To make the thumbnail index, cut the main pages as indicated by the heavy black lines in the block on the right hand side of each right-hand page, as illustrated in the diagram below:

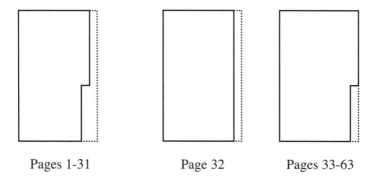

| Pages 1-31 | Page 32 | Pages 33-63 |

For the main pages it is best to make the horizontal cut first, followed by the vertical cut or cuts. Be careful when cutting the pages to make sure that you are not unintentionally cutting two pages at once.

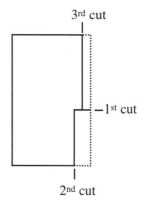

In order to have the thumbnail index visible from the finder chart, you will also have to cut these introductory pages, including the finder chart itself. Cut along the dotted line marked on the right hand edge of the right hand pages.

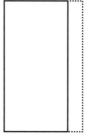

Pages v, vii, ix, xi, xiii

並 line up; ordinary HEI nara*bu*.. nami r 1* s 8	寸 tiny - SUN # r 41 s 3	勺 *shaku* SHAKU # r 20 s 3	為 do; purpose I # r 86* s 9	氷 ice - HYŌ kōri kō- hi r 85 s 5	
火 fire; Tuesday KA hi ho r 86 s 4	心 heart - SHIN kokoro r 61 s 4	必 inevitable - HITSU kanara*zu* r 61 s 5	州 state, province; sandbank SHŪ su r 47 s 6	帰 return home KI kae*ru*.. r 50* s 10	
小 small SHŌ chii*sai* ko- o- r 42 s 3	少 few - SHŌ suko*shi* suku+ r 42 s 4	劣 inferior - RETSU oto*ru* r 19 s 6	省 minister; omit; reflect upon; … SHŌ SEI habu*ku* kaeri+ r 109 s 9		
次 next - JI SHI tsugi tsu+ r 76 s 6	准 quasi-; semi; ratify JUN # r 15 s 10	凍 freeze - TŌ kō*ru* kogo+ r 15 s 10	冷 cold - REI tsume*tai* hi+ sa+ r 15 s 7		
凝 stiff; elaborate GYŌ ko*ru*.. r 15 s 16	求 seek, request KYŪ moto*meru* r 85 s 7	兆 sign, omen; trillion CHŌ kiza*shi*.. r 10 s 6	羽 feather, wing U ha hane r 124 s 6	弱 weak - JAKU yowa*i*.. r 57 s 10	
症 symptoms - SHŌ # r 104 s 10	疾 disease; speed SHITSU # r 104 s 10	疲 fatigue - HI tsuka*reru*.. r 104 s 10	病 illness BYŌ HEI yamai ya+ r 104 s 10	疫 epidemic EKI YAKU # r 104 s 9	痘 smallpox - TŌ # r 104 s 12
痛 pain TSŪ ita*mu*.. r 104 s 12	痢 diarrhea RI # r 104 s 12	痴 foolish CHI # r 104 s 13	癖 habit HEKI kuse r 104 s 18	癒 heal YU # r 104 s 18	療 treat illness RYŌ # r 104 s 17
壮 grand, strong SŌ # r 32* s 6	状 letter; state, condition JŌ # r 94 s 7	将 leader; soon SHŌ # r 41 s 10	北 north - HOKU kita r 21 s 5	兆 sign, omen; trillion CHŌ kiza*shi*.. r 10 s 6	

忙 busy - BŌ isoga*shii* r 61　s 6	快 pleasant - KAI kokoroyo*i* r 61　s 7	性 sex; nature, essence SEI SHŌ # r 61　s 8	怖 fear - FU kowa*i* r 61　s 8	恨 grudge; regret KON ura*mu..* r 61　s 9	
悼 mourn - TŌ ita*mu* r 61　s 11	慎 discreet - SHIN tsutsushi*mu* r 61　s 13	憤 indignant - FUN ikidō*ru* r 61　s 15	懐 bosom; yearn for KAI futokoro natsu+ r 61　s 16	憶 guess; recollect OKU # r 61　s 16	情 emotion; state, condition JŌ SEI nasa*ke* r 61　s 11
惜 regret - SEKI o*shii..* r 61　s 11	慌 flustered - KŌ awa*teru..* r 61　s 12	悦 joy - ETSU # r 61　s 10	憎 hate - ZŌ niku*mu..* r 61　s 14	悩 anguish, distress NŌ naya*mu..* r 61　s 10	惰 lazy - DA # r 61　s 12
恒 constant - KŌ # r 61　s 9	怪 strange, weird, spooky KAI aya*shii..* r 61　s 8	悟 enlightened - GO sato*ru* r 61　s 10	慢 arrogant; lazy MAN # r 61　s 14	慣 accustomed - KAN na*reru..* r 61　s 14	悔 repent - KAI ku*iru..* kuya+ r 61　s 9
惨 cruel; miserable SAN ZAN mije*me* r 61　s 11	愉 pleasure - YU # r 61　s 12	憾 regret - KAN # r 61　s 16			
慨 deplore - GAI # r 61　s 13	怖 fear - FU kowa*i* r 61　s 8				
灯 lamp - TŌ hi r 86　s 6	炊 cook, boil SUI ta*ku* r 86　s 8	炉 furnace, hearth RO # r 86　s 8	畑 field - # hata hatake r 102　s 9	煩 trouble, worry HAN BON wazura*u..* r 86　s 13	煙 smoke - EN kemuri kemu+ r 86　s 13
燥 dry - SŌ # r 86　s 17	焼 burn, bake SHŌ ya*keru..* r 86　s 12	爆 explode - BAKU # r 86　s 19	燃 burn, combust NEN mo*eru..* r 86　s 16		

2

汁
juice,
soup
JŪ
shiru
r 85 s 5

汗
sweat
-
KAN
ase
r 85 s 6

江
inlet,
river
KŌ
e
r 85 s 6

沖
open sea
-
CHŪ
oki
r 85 s 7

決
decide
-
KETSU
kimeru..
r 85 s 7

沈
sink (into)
-
CHIN
shizumu..
r 85 s 7

池
pond
-
CHI
ike
r 85 s 6

泌
secrete
-
HITSU HI
#
r 85 s 8

泣
weep,
cry
KYŪ
naku
r 85 s 6

汚
dirty
-
O
kitanai kega+ yogo+
r 85 s 8

油
oil
-
YU
abura
r 85 s 8

活
active
-
KATSU
#
r 85 s 9

酒
rice wine,
sake
SHU
sake saka-
r 164 s 10

沸
boiling
-
FUTSU
waku..
r 85 s 8

浄
pure
-
JŌ
#
r 85 s 9

津
harbor;
ferry
SHIN
tsu
r 85 s 9

浅
shallow
-
SEN
asai
r 85 s 9

浦
bay;
shore
HO
ura
r 85 s 10

測
measure
-
SOKU
hakaru
r 85 s 12

湖
lake
-
KO
mizuumi
r 85 s 12

潮
tide;
seawater
CHŌ
shio
r 85 s 15

漸
gradually
-
ZEN
#
r 85 s 14

瀬
shallows,
rapids
#
se
r 85 s 19

淑
graceful
-
SHUKU
#
r 85 s 11

激
violent
-
GEKI
hageshii
r 85 s 16

沢 marsh; plenty; ... TAKU sawa r 85　s 7	**泥** mud - DEI doro r 85　s 8	**涙** tears - RUI namida r 85　s 10	**漏** leak - RŌ mo*ru*.. r 85　s 14	
派 faction; send HA # r 85　s 9	**涯** limit, edge GAI # r 85　s 11	**源** source - GEN minamoto r 85　s 13	**波** waves - HA nami r 85　s 8	**渡** cross over TO wata*ru*.. r 85　s 12
河 river - KA kawa r 85　s 8	**泡** bubbles - HŌ awa r 85　s 8	**減** decrease - GEN he*ru* r 85　s 12	**滅** perish; destroy METSU horo*biru*.. r 85　s 13	
洞 cave - DŌ hora r 85　s 9	**潤** moisten - JUN uruo*u*.. uru+ r 85　s 15	**減** decrease - GEN he*ru* r 85　s 12	**滅** perish; destroy METSU horo*biru*.. r 85　s 13	**滴** drip - TEKI shizuku shitata+ r 85　s 14

1	33
2	34
3	35
4	36
5	37
6	38
7	39
8	40
9	41
10	42
11	43
12	44
13	45
14	46
15	47
16	48
17	49
18	50
19	51
20	52
21	53
22	54
23	55
24	56
25	57
26	58
27	59
28	60
29	61
30	62
31	63
32	64

■□　泊：泊　泊　泊　泊　泊

泣	済	涼	流	液	湾
weep, cry	settle up; finish	cool	current; style	fluid	bay
KYŪ	SAI	-	RYŪ RU	-	-
naku	sumu..	RYŌ	nagareru..	EKI	WAN
		suzushii..		#	#
r 85　s 8	r 85　s 11	r 85　s 11	r 85　s 10	r 85　s 11	r 85　s 12

法	溶	演	滝	滴	
law; method	melt, dissolve	performance	waterfall	drip	
HŌ HA' HO'	YŌ	-	-	-	
#	tokeru..	EN	#	TEKI	
		#	taki	shizuku shitata+	
r 85　s 8	r 85　s 13	r 85　s 14	r 85　s 13	r 85　s 14	

洗	清	漬	漆	淡	消
wash	pure	pickle	lacquer	faint, light, pale	extinguish; consume
-	-	-	-	TAN	SHŌ
SEN	SEI SHŌ	#	SHITSU	awai	kesu ki+
arau	kiyoi..	tsukeru..	urushi		
r 85　s 9	r 85　s 11	r 85　s 14	r 85　s 14	r 85　s 11	r 85　s 10

洪	港	漠	満	漢	溝
flood	harbor, port	vague; vast	full	Chinese	ditch
-	KŌ	BAKU	-	-	-
#	minato	#	MAN	KAN	KŌ
			mitasu..	#	mizo
r 85　s 9	r 85　s 12	r 85　s 13	r 85　s 12	r 85　s 13	r 85　s 13

濃	渋	渉	滞		
dense, thick, deep	astringent; hesitant	ford; connect	stay, stagnate		
NŌ	JŪ	SHŌ	TAI		
Koi	shibui..	#	todokōru		
r 85　s 16	r 85　s 11	r 85　s 11	r 85　s 13		

注	泳	浅	浦	泊	浪
pour; take note	swim	shallow	bay; shore	overnight	waves; roam
CHŪ	-	-	HO	-	RŌ
sosogu	EI	SEN	ura	HAKU	#
	oyogu	asai		tomaru..	
r 85　s 8	r 85　s 8	r 85　s 9	r 85　s 10	r 85　s 8	r 85　s 10

洋	滋	消			
ocean; Western	nourish; moist	extinguish; consume			
YŌ	JI	SHŌ			
#	#	kesu ki+			
r 85　s 9	r 85　s 12	r 85　s 10			

1	33
2	34
3	35
4	36
5	37
6	38
7	39
8	40
9	41
10	42
11	43
12	44
13	45
14	46
15	47
16	48
17	49
18	50
19	51
20	52
21	53
22	54
23	55
24	56
25	57
26	58
27	59
28	60
29	61
30	62
31	63
32	64

涙 tears - RUI namida r 85 s 10

洒 rice wine, sake - SHU sake saka- r 164 s 10

添 add to - TEN so*eru*.. r 85 s 11

漂 drift - HYŌ tadayo*u* r 85 s 14

況 conditions - KYŌ # r 85 s 8

湿 damp - SHITSU shime*ru*.. r 85 s 12

湯 hot water - TŌ yu r 85 s 12

渇 thirst - KATSU kawa*ku* r 85 s 11

混 mix - KON maze*ru*.. r 85 s 11

温 warm - ON atata*kai*.. r 85 s 12

漫 aimless; comic MAN # r 85 s 14

沼 marsh - SHŌ numa r 85 s 8

浸 soak - SHIN hita*ru*.. r 85 s 10

没 sink; die; disappear BOTSU # r 85 s 7

濁 muddy - DAKU nigo*ru*.. r 85 s 16

滑 slide; smooth KATSU sube*ru* name+ r 85 s 13

渦 whirlpool - KA uzu r 85 s 12

活 active - KATSU # r 85 s 9

浜 beach - HIN hama r 85 s 10

浮 floating - FU u*kabu*.. r 85 s 10

渓 ravine - KEI # r 85 s 11

汽 steam - KI # r 85 s 7

深 deep - SHIN fuka*i*.. r 85 s 11

海 sea - KAI umi r 85 s 9

浄 fishing - GYO RYŌ # r 85 s 14

沿 along - EN so*u* r 85 s 8

浴 bathe - YOKU a*biru*.. r 85 s 10

治 govern; heal JI CHI nao*ru*.. osa+ r 85 s 8

潟 lagoon - kata r 85 s 15

濯 wash, rinse TAKU # r 85 s 17

濫 excessive - RAN # r 85 s 18

潔 pure - KETSU isagiyo*i* r 85 s 15

潜 submerge; hide, lurk SEN mogu*ru* hiso+ r 85 s 15

澄 clear - CHŌ su*mu*.. r 85 s 15

潟 lagoon - # kata r 85 s 15

仏
Buddha;
France
BUTSU
hotoke
r9 s4

化
transform
-
KA KE
ba*keru*..
r21 s4

他
other
-
TA
#
r9 s5

仙
hermit;
fairy
SEN
#
r9 s5

作
make
-
SAKU SA
tsuku*ru*
r9 s7

付
attach
-
FU
tsu*ku*..
r9 s5

代
replace;
era; price
DAI TAI
shiro ka+ yo
r9 s5

伐
cut down
-
BATSU
#
r9 s6

伏
prostrate;
ambush
FUKU
fu*u*..
r9 s6

仕
serve
-
SHI JI
tsuka*eru*
r9 s5

休
rest
-
KYŪ
yasu*mu*..
r9 s6

体
body
-
TAI TEI
karada
r9* s7

件
affair
-
KEN
#
r9 s6

伴
accompany
-
HAN BAN
tomona*u*
r9 s7

位
rank;
approx.
I
kurai
r9 s7

依
rely on
-
I E
#
r9 s8

任
entrust;
duties
NIN
maka*seru*..
r9 s6

住
dwell
-
JŪ
su*mu*..
r9 s7

伯
aunt, uncle;
earl
HAKU
#
r9 s7

偽
deceive,
forgery
GI
nise itsuwa+
r9 s11

仲
relationship
-
CHŪ
naka
r9 s6

伸
extend,
stretch
SHIN
no*biru*..
r9 s7

使
use;
envoy
SHI
tsuka*u*
r9 s8

便
handy; mail;
excreta
BIN BEN
tayori
r9 s9

価
price,
value
KA
atai
r9 s8

信
trust;
letter
SHIN
#
r9 s9

似
resemble
-
JI
ni*ru*
r9 s7

仰
look up at;
respect
GYŌ KŌ
ao*gu* ō+
r9 s6

俳
haiku;
actor
HAI
#
r9 s10

候
season;
climate
KŌ
sōrō
r9 s10

修
learn;
mend
SHŪ SHU
osa*meru*..
r9 s10

傾
inclination
-
KEI
katamu*ku*..
r9 s13

倣
imitate
-
HŌ
nara*u*
r9 s10

側
side
-
SOKU
kawa
r9 s11

例
example
-
REI
tato*eru*
r9 s8

倒
topple;
inverted
TŌ
tao*reru*
r9 s10

働
work
-
DŌ
hatara*ku*
r9 s13

口 伍 佰 仏 佣

佐
assistant
-
SA
#
r 9 s 7

仮
temporary
-
KA KE
kari
r 9 s 6

偏
leaning,
bias
HEN
katayo*ru*
r 9 s 11

備
equip,
provide
BI
sona*eru*
r 9 s 12

何
what,
how many
KA
nani nan
r 9 s 7

伺
visit; pay
respects
SHI
ukaga*u*
r 9 s 7

値
value,
price
CHI
ne atai
r 9 s 10

健
healthy
-
KEN
suko*yaka*
r 9 s 11

個
individual;
item
KO
#
r 9 s 10

■ 伯 ： 伯 偣 伯 伯 俉

伯

佳	侍	俵	債	停
excellent	samurai; serve	bag, sack	debt	stop
-	-	-	-	-
KA	JI	HYŌ	SAI	TEI
#	samurai	tawara	#	#
r9 s8	r9 s8	r9 s10	r9 s13	r9 s11

依	位	倍	億	傍	僚
rely on	rank; approx.	multiple, -fold	100 million	beside	colleague; official
-	-	-	-	-	-
I E	I	BAI	OKU	BŌ	RYŌ
#	kurai	#	#	katawara	#
r9 s8	r9 s7	r9 s10	r9 s15	r9 s12	r9 s14

偵	偉	催	俸
spy	eminent	sponsor, organise	salary
-	-	-	-
TEI	I	SAI	HŌ
#	erai	moyōsu	#
r9 s11	r9 s12	r9 s13	r9 s10

偣

供	借	僕
offer	borrow, rent	I (male); servant
-	-	-
KYŌ KU	SHAKU	BOKU
tomo sona+	kariru	#
r9 s8	r9 s10	r9 s14

伯
伯

住	偽	伯
dwell	deceive, forgery	aunt, uncle; earl
-	-	-
JŪ	GI	HAKU
sumu..	nise itsuwa+	#
r9 s7	r9 s11	r9 s7

俉

併	僧	儀	償
combine, unite	priest; monk	ceremony	compensate
-	-	-	-
HEI	SŌ	GI	SHŌ
awaseru	#	#	tsugunau
r9 s8	r9 s13	r9 s15	r9 s17

仁 compassion - JIN NI # r9 s4	伝 transmit - DEN tsuta*eru*.. r9 s6	信 trust; letter SHIN # r9 s9	偏 leaning, bias HEN katayo*ru* r9 s11
価 price, value KA atai r9 s8	便 handy; mail; excreta BIN BEN tayori r9 s9	儒 Confucian - JU # r9 s16	優 cordial; excel; actor YŪ sugu*reru* yasa+ r9 s17
但 however; proviso # tada*shi* r9 s7	保 preserve - HO tamotsu r9 s9	促 urge on - SOKU unaga*su* r9 s9	偶 by chance; couple; doll GŪ # r9 s11
侯 marquis - KŌ # r9 s9	侵 invade - SHIN oka*su* r9 s9		
任 entrust; duties NIN maka*seru*.. r9 s6	低 low - TEI hiku*i*.. r9 s7	係 in charge; link KEI kakari kaka+ r9 s9	
侮 scorn - BU anado*ru* r9 s8	傷 wound - SHŌ kizu ita+ r9 s13	像 image - ZŌ # r9 s14	
俗 vulgar; custom ZOKU # r9 s9	倹 thrifty - KEN # r9 s10	倫 ethics - RIN # r9 s10	俊 genius - SHUN # r9 s9
傑 outstanding - KETSU # r9 s13			

■ 丨 フ 丿 丨 彳

承 Consent, be told SHŌ uketamawa*ru* r 64 s 8	水 water; Wednesday SUI mizu r 85 s 4	永 eternal - EI naga*i* r 85 s 5	氷 ice - HYŌ kōri kō- hi r 85 s 5

八 eight - HACHI ya ya'+ ya+ yō r 12 s 2	川 river - SEN kawa r 47 s 3	順 sequence; obey JUN # r 181 s 12	入 enter; put in, let in NYŪ hai*ru* i+ r 11 s 2	粛 solemn; purge SHUKU # r 129 s 11

旧 old, former KYŪ # r 72* s 5	以 by means of; datum I # r 9 s 5

行 go; do; line GYŌ KŌ AN i*ku* yu+ okona+ r 144 s 6	往 go; bygone Ō # r 60 s 8	従 follow - JŪ JU SHŌ shitaga*u*.. r 60 s 10	征 conquer; go to war SEI # r 60 s 8	律 law; rhythm RITSU RICHI # r 60 s 9	彼 he, she, they; that (yonder) HI kare kano r 60 s 8

待 await - TAI ma*tsu* r 60 s 9	徒 futile; walk; follower TO # r 60 s 10	徳 virtue - TOKU # r 60 s 14	復 restore, re- FUKU # r 60 s 12	後 after - GO KŌ nochi ushi+ ushiro ato oku+ r 60 s 9

得 gain - TOKU e*ru* u+ r 60 s 11	役 service, duty EKI YAKU # r 60 s 7	径 path; diameter KEI # r 60 s 8	徐 slowly - JO # r 60 s 10	循 circulate - JUN # r 60 s 12

街 street, arcade GAI KAI machi r 60* s 12	術 art, skill - JUTSU # r 60* s 11	衡 balance, scales KŌ # r 60* s 16	衝 collide - SHŌ # r 60* s 15	衛 guard - EI # r 60* s 16

徴 symptom; levy CHŌ # r 60 s 14	微 tiny, faint, hard to see BI # r 60 s 13	徹 thorough - TETSU # r 60 s 15	御 (honorific); control GYO GO on- r 60 s 12

■ 十 土

協	協 co-operate - KYŌ # r 24 s 8
博	extensive; Dr; gamble; … HAKU BAKU # r 24 s 12
雄	male; brave YŪ osu o r 172 s 12

地 earth, ground;
place
CHI JI
#
r 32   s 6

坪 *tsubo*;
floor area
-
#
tsubo
r 32   s 8

坑 pit
-
KŌ
#
r 32   s 7

坊 boy;
priest
BŌ BO'
#
r 32   s 7

培 cultivate
-
BAI
tsuchika*u*
r 32   s 11

境 border;
state, condition
KYŌ KEI
sakai
r 32   s 14

壊 demolish
-
KAI
kowa*reru..*
r 32   s 16

壌 soil,
earth
JŌ
#
r 32   s 16

墳 tumulus
-
FUN
#
r 32   s 15

壇 podium
-
DAN TAN
#
r 32   s 16

塔 tower
-
TŌ
#
r 32   s 12

堪 endure
-
KAN
ta*eru*
r 32   s 12

塊 lump
-
KAI
katamari
r 32   s 13

増 increase
-
ZŌ
ma*su* fu+
r 32   s 14

垣 fence
-
#
kaki
r 32   s 9

埋 bury
-
MAI
u*meru..*
r 32   s 10

堤 embankment
-
TEI
tsutsumi
r 32   s 12

場 place,
location
JŌ
ba
r 32   s 12

塩 salt
-
EN
shio
r 32*   s 13

塚 mound
-
#
tsuka
r 32   s 12

坂 slope
-
HAN
saka
r 32   s 7

塀 fence,
wall
HEI
#
r 32   s 12

堀 ditch
-
#
hori
r 32   s 11

均 equal
-
KIN
#
r 32   s 7

域 area,
zone
IKI
#
r 32   s 11

城 castle
-
JŌ
shiro
r 32   s 9

■ 犭 子 弓 巾 山 幺

犭

犯	狂	独	狭	狩	猛
crime	mad	alone; Germany	narrow	hunt	fierce
-	-	DOKU	-	-	-
HAN	KYŌ	hito*ri*	KYŌ	SHU	MŌ
oka*su*	kuru*u..*		sema*i* seba+	ka*ru..*	#
r 94 s 5	r 94 s 7	r 94 s 9	r 94 s 9	r 94 s 9	r 94 s 11

猫	猟	猶	獲	猿	獄
cat	hunting	delay; yet, still	capture	monkey	prison
-	-	YŪ	-	-	-
BYŌ	RYŌ	#	KAKU	EN	GOKU
neko	#		e*ru*	saru	#
r 94 s 11	r 94 s 11	r 94 s 12	r 94 s 16	r 94 s 13	r 94 s 14

子

孔	孤	孫
hole	solitary, orphan	grandchild
-	-	-
KŌ	KŌ	SON
#	#	mago
r 39 s 4	r 39 s 8	r 39 s 10

弓

引	弦	強	弧	張	弾
pull	string (eg of bow, harp)	strong	arc, arch	stretch	bullet; play (eg harp); ...
-	GEN	-	KO	-	DAN
IN	tsuru	KYŌ GŌ	#	CHŌ	tama hazu+ hi+
hi*ku..*		tsuyo*i..* shi+		ha*ru*	
r 57 s 4	r 57 s 8	r 57 s 11	r 57 s 9	r 57 s 11	r 57 s 12

巾

帆	帳	幅	帽
sail	notebook; curtain	width, breadth	hat
-	CHŌ	FUKU	-
HAN	#	haba	BŌ
ho			#
r 50 s 6	r 50 s 11	r 50 s 12	r 50 s 12

山

岬	岐	峡	崎	峰	峠
headland, cape	diverge	ravine	headland, cape	summit	mountain pass
#	-	-	#	-	#
misaki	KI	KYŌ	saki	HŌ	tōge
	#	#		mine	
r 46 s 8	r 46 s 7	r 46 s 9	r 46 s 11	r 46 s 10	r 46 s 9

幺

幻	幼	郷
illusion	infant	hometown; rural
-	-	KYŌ GŌ
GEN	YŌ	#
maboroshi	osana*i*	
r 52 s 4	r 52 s 5	r 163 s 11

■ 女 工 王

妃	奴	如	好	妊	
queen, empress	slave; guy	as, like, such as	good; fond of	pregnant	
HI	DO NU	JO NYO	KŌ	NIN	
#			kono*mu* su+	#	
r 38 s 6	r 38 s 5	r 38 s 6	r 38 s 6	r 38 s 7	

妹	姓	始	娘	妨	姉
younger sister	surname	begin	daughter	obstruct	elder sister
MAI	SEI SHŌ	SHI	#	BŌ	SHI
imōto	#	haji*maru..*	musume	samata*geru*	ane
r 38 s 8	r 38 s 8	r 38 s 8	r 38 s 10	r 38 s 7	r 38 s 8

妙	嫁	嫡	嬢	嫌	媒
miraculous; odd	bride; marry (a man)	legitimate heir	girl	dislike	mediation
MYŌ	KA	CHAKU	JŌ	KEN GEN	BAI
#	yome totsu+	#	#	kira*u* iya	#
r 38 s 7	r 38 s 13	r 38 s 14	r 38 s 16	r 38 s 13	r 38 s 12

婦	婿	婚	娯
woman	son in law; bridegroom	marriage	pleasure
FU	SEI	KON	GO
#	muko	#	#
r 38 s 11	r 38 s 12	r 38 s 10	r 38 s 11

娠	姫	姻
pregnant	princess	marriage
SHIN	#	IN
#	hime	#
r 38 s 10	r 38 s 10	r 38 s 9

巧	功	攻	項	頂
skillful	merit; achievement	assault	clause	summit; receive
KŌ	KŌ KU	KŌ	KŌ	CHŌ
taku*mi*	#	se*meru*	#	itadaki itada+
r 48 s 5	r 19 s 5	r 66 s 7	r 181 s 12	r 181 s 11

珠	球	現	理
pearl	ball	present, visible, existing, actual	reasoning
SHU	KYŪ	GEN	RI
#	tama	arawa*reru..*	#
r 96 s 10	r 96 s 11	r 96 s 11	r 96 s 11

珍	環	班
rare; odd	ring, circle	squad
CHIN	KAN	HAN
mezura*shii*	#	#
r 96 s 9	r 96 s 17	r 96 s 10

扣 扣 拓 抪 扠 扚

扣

打 hit - DA *utsu* r 64 s 5	**払** pay; clear away FUTSU hara*u* r 64 s 5	**扱** deal with - # atsuka*u* r 64 s 6	**拝** pray; humble HAI oga*mu* r 64 s 8	**把** grasp - HA # r 64 s 7	**押** push - Ō o*su*.. r 64 s 8
抹 erase - MATSU # r 64 s 8	**扶** aid, support FU # r 64 s 7	**挟** sandwiched - KYŌ hasa*mu*.. r 64 s 9	**抄** excerpt - SHŌ # r 64 s 7	**拙** clumsy - SETSU # r 64 s 8	**推** infer; push, put forward SUI o*su* r 64 s 11
抽 draw out, extract CHŪ # r 64 s 8	**拍** clap; beat, tempo HAKU HYŌ # r 64 s 8	**捕** catch - HO to*ru*.. tsuka+ r 64 s 10			

扣

挑 challenge - CHŌ ido*mu* r 64 s 9	**排** repel, expel; anti- HAI # r 64 s 11	**批** critique - HI # r 64 s 7	**抑** restrain, suppress YOKU osa*eru* r 64 s 7	**推** infer; push, put forward SUI o*su* r 64 s 11	**掛** hang; cost; depend; … # kakari ka+ r 64 s 11
搬 convey - HAN # r 64 s 13	**撤** withdraw - TETSU # r 64 s 15	**擬** imitate - GI # r 64 s 17			

扣

拓 clear land - TAKU # r 64 s 8	**折** fold, snap; occasion SETSU ori o+ r 64 s 7	**振** swing; shake - SHIN fu*ruu*.. r 64 s 10	**拡** expand - KAKU # r 64 s 8	**披** announce - HI # r 64 s 8	**抜** extract; omit; excel; … BATSU nu*ku*.. r 64 s 7
択 choose - TAKU # r 64 s 7	**据** install - # su*eru*.. r 64 s 11	**掘** dig - KUTSU ho*ru* r 64 s 11	**握** grasp - AKU nigi*ru* r 64 s 12		

抪 扠 扚

拒 reject - KYO koba*mu* r 64 s 8	**拠** basis - KYO KO # r 64 s 8	**拘** arrest; cling to KŌ # r 64 s 8	**抱** embrace - HŌ da*ku* ida+ kaka+ r 64 s 8

■◻ 拍

技 skill - GI waza r 64 s 7	持 hold, have JI mo*tsu* r 64 s 9	拷 torture - GŌ # r 64 s 9	指 finger; point to SHI yubi sa+ r 64 s 9	捜 search - SŌ saga*su* r 64 s 10	抗 oppose - KŌ # r 64 s 7
接 contact, touch SETSU tsu*gu* r 64 s 11	摘 pick, select TEKI tsu*mu* r 64 s 14	擁 hug; protect YŌ # r 64 s 16	擦 rub - SATSU su*reru*.. r 64 s 17	搾 squeeze - SAKU shibo*ru* r 64 s 13	控 hold back; wait; memo; … KŌ hika*eru* r 64 s 11
描 depict - BYŌ ega*ku* r 64 s 11	措 set aside; dispose of SO # r 64 s 11	搭 embark - TŌ # r 64 s 12	撲 hit - BOKU # r 64 s 15	携 carry; take part KEI tazusa*eru*.. r 64 s 13	換 exchange - KAN kae*ru*.. r 64 s 12
抄 excerpt - SHŌ # r 64 s 7	拍 clap; beat, tempo HAKU HYŌ # r 64 s 8	捕 catch - HO to*ru*.. tsuka+ r 64 s 10			
拐 kidnap; deceive KAI # r 64 s 8	損 loss, harm; fail to SON soko*nau*.. r 64 s 13	操 fidelity; operate SŌ misao ayatsu+ r 64 s 16	投 throw; send in TŌ na*geru* r 64 s 7	招 invite - SHŌ mane*ku* r 64 s 8	掃 sweep - SŌ ha*ku* r 64 s 11
担 carry; take on TAN katsu*gu* nina+ r 64 s 8	提 proffer - TEI sa*geru* r 64 s 12	揚 raise; exalt; fried YŌ a*geru*.. r 64 s 12	掲 display; pin up KEI kaka*geru* r 64 s 11	撮 photograph - SATSU to*ru* r 64 s 15	摂 ingest; regent SETSU # r 64 s 13
括 fasten; lump together KATSU # r 64 s 9	挿 insert - SŌ sa*su* r 64 s 10	採 pick, gather, harvest SAI to*ru* r 64 s 11	授 confer; teach JU sazu*keru*.. r 64 s 11	援 aid - EN # r 64 s 12	揺 shake - YŌ yu*reru*.. r 64 s 12
抵 resist; a match for TEI # r 64 s 8	探 search - TAN sagu*ru* saga+ r 64 s 11	揮 wield; command KI # r 64 s 12	拾 pick up, acquire SHŪ JŪ hiro*u* r 64 s 9	捨 discard - SHA su*teru* r 64 s 11	

1	33
2	34
3	35
4	36
5	37
6	38
7	39
8	40
9	41
10	42
11	43
12	44
13	45
14	46
15	47
16	48
17	49
18	50
19	51
20	52
21	53
22	54
23	55
24	56
25	57
26	58
27	59
28	60
29	61
30	62
31	63
32	64

札 chit, tag, banknote - SATSU fuda r75 s5	朴 simple - BOKU # r75 s6	材 timber; raw material ZAI # r75 s7	村 village - SON mura r75 s7	林 woods - RIN hayashi r75 s8	株 stocks, shares; stump # kabu r75 s10
棟 building; roof ridge TŌ mune muna- r75 s12	枚 sheet (of paper) MAI # r75 s8	桟 plank; jetty; bridge SAN # r75 s10	杉 Japanese cedar # sugi r75 s7	権 authority - KEN GON # r75 s15	
朽 decay - KYŪ kuchiru r75 s6	杯 cup, glass HAI sakazuki r75 s8	柄 handle; nature HEI gara e r75 s9	机 desk - KI tsukue r75 s6	相 mutual; minister SŌ SHŌ ai- r109 s9	根 root - KON ne r75 s10
桃 peach - TŌ momo r75 s10	柳 willow - RYŪ yanagi r75 s9	棚 shelf - # tana r75 s12	概 in general; roughly GAI # r75 s14	樹 tree - JU # r75 s16	極 extremes - KYOKU GOKU kiwami.. r75 s12
析 analyze - SEKI # r75 s8	板 board - HAN BAN ita r75 s8	植 plant - SHOKU ueru.. r75 s12			
械 apparatus, machine KAI # r75 s11	機 machine; opportunity KI hata r75 s16				
枢 pivotal - SŪ # r75 s8	欄 railing; column (in newspaper) RAN # r75 s20				

■▮ 相

日

柱	核

柱
pillar
-
CHŪ
hashira
r 75　s 9

核
nucleus
-
KAKU
#
r 75　s 10

校
school
-
KŌ
#
r 75　s 10

枯
wither
-
KO
ka*reru*..
r 75　s 9

枝
branch
-
SHI
eda
r 75　s 8

枠
frame
-
#
waku
r 75　s 8

植
plant
-
SHOKU
u*eru*..
r 75　s 12

棺
coffin
-
KAN
#
r 75　s 12

棒
rod
-
BŌ
#
r 75　s 12

桜
cherry (tree,
blossom)
Ō
sakura
r 75　s 10

楼
tower
-
RŌ
#
r 75　s 13

桟
plank; jetty;
bridge
SAN
#
r 75　s 10

棋
game of *go*,
shogi
KI
#
r 75　s 12

横
side
-
Ō
yoko
r 75　s 15

構
build;
care about
KŌ
kama*eru*
r 75　s 14

槽
tank,
tub
SŌ
#
r 75　s 15

模
imitate
-
MO BO
#
r 75　s 14

様
way, manner;
Mr, Mrs
YŌ
sama
r 75　s 14

杉
Japanese
cedar
#
sugi
r 75　s 7

格
state,
condition
KAKU KŌ
#
r 75　s 10

梅
ume, plum,
apricot
BAI
ume
r 75　s 10

杯
cup,
glass
HAI
sakazuki
r 75　s 8

柄
handle;
nature
HEI
gara e
r 75　s 9

標
sign
-
HYŌ
#
r 75　s 15

極
extremes
-
KYOKU GOKU
kiwa*mi*..
r 75　s 12

橋
bridge
-
KYŌ
hashi
r 75　s 16

松
pine
tree
SHŌ
matsu
r 75　s 8

栓
stopper
-
SEN
#
r 75　s 10

検
examine
-
KEN
#
r 75　s 12

禾 米 耒

禾

私	利	秋	秒	秘	科
I; private	profit, benefit, (loan) interest	fall (autumn)	second (unit of time)	secret	(academic) subject
-				-	
SHI	RI	SHŪ	BYŌ	HI	KA
watakushi	ki*ku*	aki	#	hi*meru*	#
r 115 s 7	r 18 s 7	r 115 s 9	r 115 s 9	r 115 s 10	r 115 s 9

称	秩	稚	租	和	
name, title	order, system	childish; infant	tax, tribute, levy	harmony; Japan	
-					
SHŌ	CHITSU	CHI	SO	WA O	
#	#	#	#	nago*mu*.. yawa+	
r 115 s 10	r 115 s 10	r 115 s 13	r 115 s 10	r 30 s 8	

種	稲	穏	税	移	程
seed; type of	rice plant	calm	tax	move, transfer	extent
			-		-
SHU	TŌ	ON	ZEI	I	TEI
tane	ine ina-	oda*yaka*	#	utsu*ru*..	hodo
r 115 s 14	r 115 s 14	r 115 s 16	r 115 s 12	r 115 s 11	r 115 s 12

稼	稿	積	穂	穫	釈
earnings	manuscript	accumulate	tip of; ear of grain	harvest	explain
-	-	-			-
KA	KŌ	SEKI	SUI	KAKU	SHAKU
kase*gu*	#	tsu*mu*..	ho	#	#
r 115 s 15	r 115 s 15	r 115 s 16	r 115 s 15	r 115 s 18	r 165 s 11

米

料	粗	粘	粒	粋	粉
fee; materials	coarse	sticky	particle, grain of	pure, elegant	flour, powder
RYŌ	-				
#	SO	NEN	RYŪ	SUI	FUN
	ara*i*	neba*ru*	tsubu	#	kona ko
r 68 s 10	r 119 s 11	r 119 s 11	r 119 s 11	r 119 s 10	r 119 s 10

精	糧	粧	糖	釈	
spirit, essence	provisions	cosmetics	sugar	explain	
		-	-	-	
SEI SHŌ	RYŌ RŌ	SHŌ	TŌ	SHAKU	
#	kate	#	#	#	
r 119 s 14	r 119 s 18	r 119 s 12	r 119 s 16	r 165 s 11	

耒

耗	耕	栽
use up, wear out	plow	plant
	-	-
MŌ KŌ	KŌ	SAI
#	tagaya*su*	#
r 127 s 10	r 127 s 10	r 75 s 10

■ ネ ネ 方 牛 矢

礼	祈	祉	社	祥	禅
etiquette	pray	welfare	company, firm; society; shrine	auspicious	Zen
-	KI	SHI	SHA	SHŌ	ZEN
REI RAI	inoru	#	yashiro	#	#
r 113 s 5	r 113 s 7	r 113 s 7	r 113 s 7	r 113 s 7	r 113 s 7

祝	視	祖	神	福	禍
celebrate	look at, watch	ancestor	god	blessing, good fortune	calamity
-	SHI	SO	SHIN JIN	FUKU	KA
SHUKU SHŪ	#	#	kami kan- kō	#	#
iwau	r 147 s 11	r 113 s 7	r 113 s 7	r 113 s 7	r 113 s 7
r 113 s 7					

補	被	初
compensate; replenish	undergo, -ee; wear, cover	first time
HO	HI	SHO
oginau	kōmoru	hatsu- ui- haji+ -so+
r 145 s 12	r 145 s 0	r 18 s 7

裕	裸	褐	複	襟
abundant	naked	brown	compound; duplicate	collar, neck
-	-	-	FUKU	KIN
YŪ	RA	KATSU	#	eri
#	hadaka	#	r 145 s 14	r 145 s 18
r 145 s 12	r 145 s 13	r 145 s 13		

放	旅	施	旋	族	旗
set free; emit	travel	do; donate	rotation	family	flag
HŌ	-	SHI SE	SEN	ZOKU	KI
hanatsu..	RYO	hodokusu	#	#	hata
r 66 s 8	tabi	r 70 s 9	r 70 s 11	r 70 s 11	r 70 s 14
	r 70 s 10				

加
add; join in
KA
kuwaeru..
r 19 s 5

牧	物	牲	特	犠
pasture	thing	sacrifice	special	sacrifice
-	-	-	-	-
BOKU	BUTSU MOTSU	SEI	TOKU	GI
maki	mono	#	#	#
r 93 s 8	r 93 s 8	r 93 s 9	r 93 s 10	r 93 s 17

知	短	矯
know	short	rectify
-	-	-
CHI	TAN	KYŌ
shiru	mijikai	tameru
r 111 s 8	r 111 s 12	r 111 s 17

1	33
2	34
3	35
4	36
5	37
6	38
7	39
8	40
9	41
10	42
11	43
12	44
13	45
14	46
15	47
16	48
17	49
18	50
19	51
20	52
21	53
22	54
23	55
24	56
25	57
26	58
27	59
28	60
29	61
30	62
31	63
32	64

糸 糸□ 糸□ 糸□ 糸□ 糸□ 糸□

糸□

糾	紅	紀	約	紙	級
inquire; twist	crimson	era; chronicle	pledge; approx.	paper	grade, rank
KYŪ	KŌ KU	KI	YAKU	SHI	KYŪ
#	kurenai beni	#	#	kami	#
r 120 s 9	r 120 s 9	r 120 s 9	r 120 s 9	r 120 s 10	r 120 s 9

紺	紳	練	純	納
dark blue	gentleman	training	pure	pay; obtain; store; supply
KON	SHIN	REN	JUN	NŌ NA NA' NAN TŌ
#	#	neru	#	osameru..
r 120 s 11	r 120 s 11	r 120 s 14	r 120 s 10	r 120 s 10

組	細	紋	紡	幻	幼
group, union	thin, fine	family crest	spin (yarn)	illusion	infant
SO	SAI	MON	BŌ	GEN	YŌ
kumi ku+	hosoi.. koma+	#	tsumugu	maboroshi	osanai
r 120 s 11	r 120 s 11	r 120 s 10	r 120 s 10	r 52 s 4	r 52 s 5

糸□

維	縦	郷
fiber; upkeep	vertical; selfish	hometown; rural
I	JŪ	KYŌ GŌ
#	tate	#
r 120 s 14	r 120 s 16	r 163 s 11

糸□

編
knit, edit
HEN
amu
r 120 s 15

糸□

継	縫
inherit	sew
KEI	HŌ
tsugu	nuu
r 120 s 13	r 120 s 16

糸□

約	繊	織
pledge; approx.	fine, slender; fiber	weave
YAKU	SEN	SHIKI SHOKU
#	#	oru
r 120 s 9	r 120 s 17	r 120 s 18

糸□

綱	網	納
rope; gist	net	pay; obtain; store; supply
KŌ	MŌ	NŌ NA NA' NAN TŌ
tsuna	ami	osameru..
r 120 s 14	r 120 s 14	r 120 s 10

■ 絽日

日

紡	紋	絞	統	締	縮
spin (yarn)	family crest	strangle	unite; rule, govern	tight; tie up	shrink
-	-	-	-	-	-
BŌ	MON	KŌ	TŌ	TEI	SHUKU
tsumu*gu*	#	shibo*ru* shi+	su*beru*	shi*meru*..	chiji*maru*..
r 120 s 10	r 120 s 10	r 120 s 12	r 120 s 12	r 120 s 15	r 120 s 17

結	続	緒	緯	績
tie, bind	continue	beginning; clue; cord	horizontal	achievement
KETSU	ZOKU	SHO CHO	-	-
musu*bu* yu+	tsuzu*ku*..	o	I	SEKI
r 120 s 12	r 120 s 13	r 120 s 14	#	#
			r 120 s 16	r 120 s 17

綿	線	縛	繕
cotton	line	tie, bind	repair
-	-	BAKU	ZEN
MEN	SEN	shiba*ru*	tsukoro*u*
wata	#	r 120 s 16	r 120 s 18
r 120 s 14	r 120 s 15		

緑	縁	絹	縄	繰	編
green	edge; relation	silk	rope	reel, wind; move along; ...	knit, edit
-	-	-	-	#	HEN
RYOKU ROKU	EN	KEN	JŌ	ku*ru*	a*mu*
midori	fuchi	kinu	nawa	r 120 s 19	r 120 s 15
r 120 s 14	r 120 s 15	r 120 s 13	r 120 s 15		

紹	経	終	絡	絶
introduce	pass through; economics; ...	end	entwine; link	discontinue; die out
-	KEI KYŌ	-	RAKU	ZETSU
SHŌ	he*ru*	SHŪ	kara*mu*..	tae*ru*..
#	r 120 s 11	o*waru*..	r 120 s 12	r 120 s 12
r 120 s 11		r 120 s 11		

緩	紛	総	給	絵
slack	confuse	general; whole	supply, pay	picture
-	-	SŌ	KYŪ	E KAI
KAN	FUN	#	#	#
yuru*mu*..	magi*reru*..	r 120 s 14	r 120 s 12	r 120 s 12
r 120 s 15	r 120 s 10			

■▮ ▯ 日

口

叫	吐	吹	味	咲	呼
shout	spit; vomit	blow	taste	bloom	call
-	-	-	-	#	-
KYŌ	TO	SUI	MI	saku	KO
sakebu	haku	fuku	aji aji+		yobu
r 30 s 6	r 30 s 6	r 30 s 7	r 30 s 8	r 30 s 9	r 30 s 8

吸	唯	鳴	唱	喝
suck, inhale	only, sole	(animal) cry, howl; sound	chant	shout
KYŪ	YUI I	MEI	SHŌ	KATSU
suu	#	naku..	tonaeru	#
r 30 s 6	r 30 s 11	r 196 s 14	r 30 s 11	r 30 s 11

吟	唆	喚	嘆	噴
recite	incite	call	sigh, grief	erupt
-	-	-	-	-
GIN	SA	KAN	TAN	FUN
#	sosonokasu	#	nageku..	fuku
r 30 s 7	r 30 s 10	r 30 s 12	r 30 s 13	r 30 s 15

嘱	嚇	喫	可	句
entrust	threaten	eat, drink, smoke	possible; approve	phrase
-	-			
SHOKU	KAKU	KITSU	KA	KU
#	#	#	#	#
r 30 s 15	r 30 s 17	r 30 s 12	r 30 s 5	r 30 s 5

日

昨	明	映
yesterday, past	bright; next	reflect, shine; movie
SAKU	MYŌ MEI	EI
#	aku.. aki+ aka+	utsusu.. ha+
r 72 s 9	r 72 s 8	r 72 s 9

時	晩	暗	暁	晴	暖
time; hour	evening, late	dark, hidden	daybreak	fine weather	warm
JI	BAN	AN	GYŌ	SEI	DAN
toki	#	kurai	akatsuki	hareru..	atatakai..
r 72 s 10	r 72 s 12	r 72 s 13	r 72 s 12	r 72 s 12	r 72 s 13

昭	暇	曜	旬	的
clear, bright	leisure	day of week	10 day period	target; -like
SHŌ	KA	YŌ	JUN	TEKI
#	hima	#	#	mato
r 72 s 9	r 72 s 13	r 72 s 18	r 72 s 6	r 106 s 8

■□ 田 目 貝

町	town, part of town CHŌ machi r 102 s 7
畔	shore - HAN # r 102 s 10
略	abbreviate - RYAKU # r 102 s 11

眼	eye - GAN GEN manako r 109 s 11
眠	sleep - MIN nemuru.. r 109 s 10
睡	sleep - SUI # r 109 s 13
瞬	moment; blink - SHUN matataku r 109 s 18
眺	view, look at - CHŌ nagameru r 109 s 11
助	help - JO suke tasu+ r 19 s 7

則	rule - SOKU # r 18 s 9
財	finance; property - ZAI SAI # r 154 s 10
敗	be defeated - HAI yabureru r 66 s 11

貯	store up - CHO # r 154 s 12
賠	compensate - BAI # r 154 s 15
賜	give, bestow - SHI tamawaru r 154 s 15
贈	gift - ZŌ SŌ okuru r 154 s 18
購	buy - KŌ # r 154 s 17

販	sell, trade HAN # r 154 s 11
賄	bribe; pay for WAI makanau r 154 s 13
賊	robber - ZOKU # r 154 s 13
賦	tax; payment FU # r 154 s 15
期	term; expect KI # r 130* s 12
欺	deceive, cheat GI azamuku r 76 s 12

歹

列	殊	残	
row, line	special	remain; cruel	
RETSU	SHU	ZAN	
#	koto	nokosu..	
r 18 s 6	r 78 s 10	r 78 s 10	

殉	殖	死	外
martyr	increase, multiply	death	outside; foreign
-	-	-	-
JUN	SHOKU	SHI	GAI GE
#	fueru..	shinu	soto hoka hazu+
r 78 s 10	r 78 s 12	r 78 s 6	r 36 s 5

石

砂	砕	硝	硫	破	
sand	pulverize	gunpowder; nitric-	sulfur	break, ruin	
-	-	-	-	-	
SA SHA	SAI	SHŌ	RYŪ	HA	
suna	kudakeru..	#	#	yaburu..	
r 112 s 9	r 112 s 9	r 112 s 12	r 112 s 12	r 112 s 10	

研	硬				
hone, grind, polish	hard, firm				
KEN	KŌ				
togu	katai				
r 112 s 9	r 112 s 12				

砲	碑	礁	確	磁	礎
cannon	monument	reef	certainty	magnet; porcelain	cornerstone
-	-	-	-	-	-
HŌ	HI	SHŌ	KAKU	JI	SO
#	#	#	tashka..	#	ishizue
r 112 s 10	r 112 s 14	r 112 s 17	r 112 s 15	r 112 s 14	r 112 s 18

酉

配	酢	酌	酷	酪	酔
distribute	vinegar	serve wine	severe	dairy produce	drunk
-	-	-	-	-	-
HAI	SAKU	SHAKU	KOKU	RAKU	SUI
kubaru	su	#	#	#	you
r 164 s 10	r 164 s 12	r 164 s 10	r 164 s 14	r 164 s 13	r 164 s 11

酵	酸	醜	醸	酬	
ferment	acid	ugly	brew	reward	
-	-	-	-	-	
KŌ	SAN	SHŪ	JŌ	SHŪ	
#	sui	minikui	kamosu	#	
r 164 s 14	r 164 s 14	r 164 s 17	r 164 s 20	r 164 s 13	

距	践	跡	跳	路
distance	carry out, put into practice	vestige, trace, footprints	jump	road, way
-	SEN	SEKI	CHŌ	RO
KYO	#	ato	tobu ha+	-ji
#	r 157 s 13	r 157 s 13	r 157 s 13	r 157 s 13
r 157 s 12				

踏	踊	躍
tread, stand on	dance	leap
TŌ	-	-
fumu..	YŌ	YAKU
r 157 s 15	odoru..	odoru
	r 157 s 14	r 157 s 21

蚊	蛇
mosquito	snake
-	-
#	JA DA
ka	hebi
r 142 s 10	r 142 s 11

軒	転	軟	軌	軸
eaves	revolve; overturn	soft	track, orbit	axle, axis
-	TEN	-	KI	JIKU
KEN	korobu..	NAN	#	#
noki	r 159 s 11	yawaraka..	r 159 s 9	r 159 s 12
r 159 s 10		r 159 s 11		

軽	較	轄	輪	輸	載
light, slight	compare	jurisdiction, control	wheel, ring	transport	load; publish
KEI	KAKU	KATSU	RIN	YU	SAI
karui karo+	#	#	wa	#	noru..
r 159 s 12	r 159 s 13	r 159 s 17	r 159 s 15	r 159 s 16	r 159 s 13

朝	乾	幹
morning; dynasty	dry	trunk, main part
CHŌ	-	KAN
asa	KAN	miki
r 130* s 12	kawaku..	r 51 s 13
	r 5 s 11	

取	恥	聴	職	敢
take	shame; shy	listen	employment	daring
-	CHI	-	-	KAN
SHU	haji ha+	CHŌ	SHOKU	#
toru	r 61 s 10	kiku	#	r 66 s 12
r 29 s 8		r 128 s 17	r 128 s 18	

邪	雅	刑	形
wicked	elegant	punishment	shape
-	-	-	-
JA	GA	KEI	KEI GYŌ
#	#	#	katachi kata
r 163 s 8	r 172 s 13	r 18 s 6	r 59 s 7

計 compute; plan - KEI haka*ru*.. r 149 s 9	討 attack - TŌ u*tsu* r 149 s 10	記 write down - KI shiru*su* r 149 s 10	訳 translate - YAKU wake r 149 s 11	訂 revise - TEI # r 149 s 9	託 entrust - TAKU # r 149 s 10
許 permit - KYO yuru*su* r 149 s 11	詐 deceive - SA # r 149 s 12	証 proof, evidence SHŌ # r 149 s 12	訪 visit - HŌ tazu*neru* otozu+ r 149 s 11	詠 recite or write poetry EI yo*mu* r 149 s 12	該 aforesaid; applicable GAI # r 149 s 13
評 appraise - HYŌ # r 149 s 12	詳 detailed - SHŌ kuwa*shii* r 149 s 13				
訓 instruct - KUN # r 149 s 10	謝 thank; apology SHA ayama*ru* r 149 s 17				
訴 sue; appeal SO utta*eru* r 149 s 12					
誕 birth - TAN # r 149 s 15					
討 attack - TŌ u*tsu* r 149 s 10	詞 word - SHI # r 149 s 12	試 try - SHI tame*su* kokoro+ r 149 s 13	誠 sincerity - SEI makoto r 149 s 13	識 discern - SHIKI # r 149 s 19	
誠 sincerity - SEI makoto r 149 s 13	調 tone; tune; inspect CHŌ shira*beru* totono+ r 149 s 15				

詰
cram;
rebuke
KITSU
tsu*mu*..
r 149　s 13

請
request
-
SEI SHIN
ko*u* u+
r 149　s 15

詩
poem
-
SHI
#
r 149　s 13

誌
magazine,
journal
SHI
#
r 149　s 14

読
read
-
DOKU TOKU TŌ
yo*mu*
r 149　s 14

訪
visit
-
HŌ
tazu*neru* otozu+
r 149　s 11

該
aforesaid;
applicable
GAI
#
r 149　s 13

諸
various
-
SHO
#
r 149　s 15

誇
boast
-
KO
hoko*ru*
r 149　s 13

談
talk
-
DAN
#
r 149　s 15

譲
concede
-
JŌ
yuzu*ru*
r 149　s 20

諾
consent
-
DAKU
#
r 149　s 15

謹
respectful
-
KIN
tsutsushi*mu*
r 149　s 17

護
protect
-
GO
#
r 149　s 20

謀
conspire
-
BŌ MU
haka*ru*
r 149　s 16

講
lecture
-
KŌ
#
r 149　s 17

詠
recite or
write poetry
EI
yo*mu*
r 149　s 12

詳
detailed
-
SHŌ
kuwa*shii*
r 149　s 13

説
explanation
-
SETSU ZEI
to*ku*
r 149　s 14

譜
written
record
FU
#
r 149　s 19

謙
modest
-
KEN
#
r 149　s 17

議
debate
-
GI
#
r 149　s 20

誤
mistake
-
GO
aya*maru*
r 149　s 14

謁
audience
with
ETSU
#
r 149　s 15

課
section;
lesson
KA
#
r 149　s 15

設
establish
-
SETSU
mō*keru*
r 149　s 11

語
language,
word; talk
GO
kata*ru*..
r 149　s 14

詔
imperial
edict
SHŌ
mikotonori
r 149　s 12

認
recognize
-
NIN
mito*meru*
r 149　s 14

託
entrust
-
TAKU
#
r 149　s 10

話
speak;
tale
WA
hanashi hana+
r 149　s 13

誘
entice
-
YŪ
saso*u*
r 149　s 14

謡
song,
chant
YŌ
uta*u*
r 149　s 16

訟
sue,
accuse
SHŌ
#
r 149　s 11

診
diagnose
-
SHIN
mi*ru*
r 149　s 12

論
theory
-
RON
#
r 149　s 15

諭
admonish
-
YU
sato*su*
r 149　s 16

諮
consult
-
SHI
haka*ru*
r 149　s 16

■◻ 月 舟

月

肌	肝	肺	肪	豚	肥
skin	liver	lungs	animal fat	pig	fatten, enrich
-	-	-	BŌ	-	HI
#	KAN	HAI	#	TON	koe ko+
hada	kimo	#		buta	
r 130 s 6	r 130 s 7	r 130 s 9	r 130 s 8	r 152 s 11	r 130 s 8

肢	脂	胎	腹	膜	腕
limb	animal fat	womb	abdomen	membrane	arm; skill
-	SHI	-	-	-	WAN
SHI	abura	TAI	FUKU	MAKU	ude
#		#	hara	#	
r 130 s 8	r 130 s 10	r 130 s 9	r 130 s 13	r 130 s 14	r 130 s 12

脱	朕	脳
remove; escape	I (imperial)	brain
DATSU	CHIN	-
nugu..	#	NŌ
r 130 s 11	r 130* s 10	#
		r 130 s 11

勝	謄	騰	臓
victory; surpass	copy	(price) rise	entrails
SHŌ	-	-	ZŌ
katsu masa+	TŌ	TŌ	#
r 19 s 12	#	#	r 130 s 19
	r 149 s 17	r 187 s 20	

服	腸	腰	胆	脹
clothes; obey	intestine	loins, hips	gall bladder	expand
FUKU	-	YŌ	TAN	-
#	CHŌ	koshi	#	CHŌ
r 130* s 8	#			#
	r 130 s 13	r 130 s 13	r 130 s 9	r 130 s 12

脈	胴	胞	胸	脚	膨
vein, pulse	torso	placenta	bosom	leg, foot	swell
MYAKU	-	-	-	KYAKU KYA	-
#	DŌ	HŌ	KYŌ	ashi	BŌ
	#	#	mune muna-		fukureru..
r 130 s 10	r 130 s 10	r 130 s 9	r 130 s 10	r 130 s 11	r 130 s 16

舟

舶	航	般	船	艇	艦
large ship	navigate	sort, kind; time	ship	boat	warship
-	-	-	-	-	-
HAKU	KŌ	HAN	SEN	TEI	KAN
#	#	#	fune funa-	#	#
r 137 s 11	r 137 s 10	r 137 s 10	r 137 s 11	r 137 s 13	r 137 s 21

阻	限	隅	陣	陳	防
obstruct	limit	corner	camp; formation	exhibit, declare	prevent
-	-	-	-	-	-
SO	GEN	GŪ	JIN	CHIN	BŌ
haba*mu*	kagi*ru*	sumi	#	#	fuse*gu*
r 170 s 8	r 170 s 9	r 170 s 12	r 170 s 10	r 170 s 11	r 170 s 7

陪	院	陸	陵	障	
attend on	institute	land	imperial tomb	obstacle	
-	-	-	RYŌ	-	
BAI	IN	RIKU	misasagi	SHŌ	
#	#	#		sawa*ru*	
r 170 s 11	r 170 s 10	r 170 s 11	r 170 s 11	r 170 s 14	

隊	隣				
crew, gang	neighbor				
TAI	-				
#	RIN				
	tonari tona+				
r 170 s 12	r 170 s 16				

陽	隔	隠	陥	降	隆
sun; positive	apart; alternate, every other	conceal	collapse, cave in; trap	descend	prosper; high
YŌ	KAKU	-	KAN	KŌ	RYŪ
#	heda*teru*..	IN	ochii*ru* otoshii+	o*riru*.. fu+	#
r 170 s 12	r 170 s 13	kaku*reru*..	r 170 s 10	r 170 s 10	r 170 s 11
		r 170 s 14			

除	険	陰	陛	階	際
remove	steep; risk	shade; negative	Your Majesty	floor, story; stairs; rank	occasion; edge
-	KEN	IN	HEI	KAI	SAI
JO JI	kewa*shii*	kage kage+	#	#	kiwa
nozo*ku*	r 170 s 11	r 170 s 11	r 170 s 10	r 170 s 12	r 170 s 14
r 170 s 10					

附	随	陶			
attach	follow	pottery			
-	-	-			
FU	ZUI	TŌ			
#	#	#			
r 170 s 8	r 170 s 12	r 170 s 11			

即	既	門
Immediate; namely; i.e.	already	gate, door
SOKU	-	MON
#	KI	kado
r 26 s 7	sude	r 169 s 8
	r 71* s 10	

郎	朗	帥	師
man	cheerful; bright, clear	commander	teacher; army
-	RŌ	-	SHI
RŌ	hoga*raka*	SUI	#
#	r 130* s 10	#	r 50 s 10
r 163 s 9		r 50 s 9	

1	33
2	34
3	35
4	36
5	37
6	38
7	39
8	40
9	41
10	42
11	43
12	44
13	45
14	46
15	47
16	48
17	49
18	50
19	51
20	52
21	53
22	54
23	55
24	56
25	57
26	58
27	59
28	60
29	61
30	62
31	63
32	64

◨ 金 食

金

針	鉢	鈍	鉄	銑	銃
needle	bowl, pot	dull, slow	iron	pig iron	gun
-	HACHI HATSU	DON	-	-	-
SHIN	#	nibu*i*	TETSU	SEN	JŪ
hari			#	#	#
r 167 s 10	r 167 s 13	r 167 s 12	r 167 s 13	r 167 s 14	r 167 s 14

錬	銀	錘	銭	鋳	録
refine; training	silver	spindle	coin	cast metal	record
REN	-	-	-	CHŪ	-
#	GIN	SUI	SEN	i*ru*	ROKU
	#	tsumu	zeni		#
r 167 s 16	r 167 s 14	r 167 s 16	r 167 s 14	r 167 s 15	r 167 s 16

錠	銑	鏡	鐘	鎮	錯
lock; pill	pig iron	mirror	bell	suppress	confused
JŌ	-	-	-	-	SAKU
#	SEN	KYŌ	SHŌ	CHIN	#
	#	kagami	kane	shizu*meru..*	
r 167 s 16	r 167 s 14	r 167 s 19	r 167 s 20	r 167 s 18	r 167 s 16

銘	鉛	鈴	鋭	鎖	
inscription	lead (the metal)	bell	sharp	chain; lock up	
-	EN	REI RIN	-	SA	
MEI	namari	suzu	EI	kusari	
#			surudo*i*		
r 167 s 14	r 167 s 13	r 167 s 13	r 167 s 15	r 167 s 18	

鉱	釣	銅	鋼	鍛	鑑
ore, mine	fishing; hanging	copper	steel	forge metal; training	model; take heed
KŌ	CHŌ	-	-	TAN	KAN
#	tsu*ru*	DŌ	KŌ	kita*eru*	#
		#	hagane		
r 167 s 13	r 167 s 11	r 167 s 14	r 167 s 16	r 167 s 17	r 167 s 23

食

飢	飯	飲	飾	館
hunger, starve	meal, cooked rice	drink	decorate	public building
KI	HAN	-	-	KAN
u*eru*	meshi	IN	SHOKU	#
		no*mu*	kaza*ru*	
r 184 s 10	r 184 s 12	r 184 s 12	r 184 s 13	r 184 s 16

飼	飽	餓
raise, breed	sated	starve
SHI	-	-
ka*u*	HŌ	GA
	a*kiru..*	#
r 184 s 13	r 184 s 13	r 184 s 15

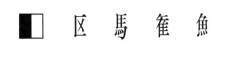

欧	殴		
Europe	assault		
-	-		
Ō	Ō		
#	naguru		
r 76 s 8	r 79 s 8		

駅	駐	駄	駆
station	reside, stay	no good, poor quality	spur on; drive; expel
-	-	-	KU
EKI	CHŪ	DA	karu..
#	#	#	
r 187 s 14	r 187 s 15	r 187 s 14	r 187 s 14

騎	験	騒
ride a horse	examine; effect	noise, clamor
KI	KEN GEN	SŌ
#	#	sawagu
r 187 s 18	r 187 s 18	r 187 s 18

勧	歓	観
advise; encourage	delight	view; observe
KAN	KAN	KAN
susumeru	#	#
r 19 s 13	r 76 s 15	r 147 s 18

鯨	鮮	触	解
whale	fresh, vivid	touch	unravel; solve
-	-	-	KAI GE
GEI	SEN	SHOKU	toku..
kujira	azayaka	sawa fu+	
r 195 s 19	r 195 s 17	r 148 s 13	r 148 s 13

	対 oppose; pair TAI TSUI # r 41 s 7	効 effective - KŌ ki*ku* r 19 s 8	郊 outskirts, suburbs - KŌ # r 163 s 9	端 edge; end; beginning; ... TAN hashi hata ha r 117 s 14	劾 denounce, impeach GAI # r 19 s 8
文 立 交 亥					
亩 京	畝 ridge *se* # une se r 102 s 10	就 start to - SHŪ JU tsu*ku*.. r 43 s 12	郭 enclosure - KAKU # r 163 s 11		
古 青	故 old; dead; intent KO yue r 66 s 9	静 quiet - SEI JŌ shizu shizu+ r 174 s 14			
東 半 求 类	勅 imperial edict CHOKU # r 19 s 9	頼 rely on; request RAI tayo*ru* tano+ r 181* s 16	判 judge HAN BAN # r 18 s 7	救 rescue - KYŪ suku*u* r 66 s 11	類 sort, kind RUI # r 181 s 18
音 音 竞	剖 dissect - BŌ # r 18 s 10	部 section - BU # r 163 s 11	韻 rhyme, tone IN # r 180 s 19	競 compete - KYŌ KEI kiso*u* se+ r 117 s 20	
亲 彦 离 客	親 parent, kin; intimate SHIN oya shita+ r 147 s 16	新 new - SHIN nii- atara+ ara+ r 69 s 13	顔 face - GAN kao r 181 s 18	離 separation RI hana*reru*.. r 172 s 18	額 sum; frame; forehead GAKU hitai r 181 s 18
去 赤 圭 幸	却 reject; exclude KYAKU # r 26 s 7	赦 pardon, forgive SHA # r 155 s 11	封 seal up FŪ HŌ # r 41 s 9	報 report; reward HŌ muku*iru* r 32 s 12	執 grasp; carry out SHITSU SHŪ to*ru* r 32 s 11
耂 壴 売 橐	款 clause; cordial KAN # r 76 s 12	隷 servant, subordinate REI # r 171 s 16	鼓 drum KO tsuzumi r 207 s 13	殻 shell KAKU kara r 79 s 11	穀 grain, cereal KOKU # r 115 s 14

■

七 上 ⺕

未 步 歯

其 莫

片 川 左

⺕ 丰 夫

朵 𦥑

𦣻

并 光 単

以	切	比	北
by means of; datum	cut	compare	north
I	SETSU SAI	HI	HOKU
#	ki*ru*..	kura*beru*	kita
r 9 s 5	r 18 s 4	r 81 s 4	r 21 s 5

叔	雌	頻	齢
aunt, uncle	female	frequent	age
SHUKU	SHI	HIN	REI
#	mesu me	#	#
r 29 s 8	r 172 s 14	r 181 s 17	r 211 s 17

収	欺	期	難
obtain; seize; collect; ...	deceive, cheat	term; expect	difficult
SHŪ	GI	KI	NAN
osa*meru*..	azamu*ku*	#	kata*i* muzuka+
r 29* s 5	r 76 s 12	r 130* s 12	r 172 s 18

加	版	順	雄
add; join in	printing	sequence; obey	male; brave
KA	HAN	JUN	YŪ
kuwa*eru*..	#	#	osu o
r 19 s 5	r 91 s 8	r 181 s 12	r 172 s 12

兆	非	邦	規
sign, omen; trillion	un-, non-	homeland; Japan	regulation
CHŌ	HI	HŌ	KI
kiza*shi*..	#	#	#
r 10 s 6	r 175 s 8	r 163 s 7	r 147 s 11

郷	雑	能
hometown; rural	miscellany	ability; *Noh* play
KYŌ GŌ	ZATSU ZŌ	NŌ
#	#	#
r 163 s 11	r 172 s 14	r 130 s 10

的	帥	師
target; -like	commander	teacher; army
TEKI	SUI	SHI
mato	#	#
r 106 s 8	r 50 s 9	r 50 s 10

射	瓶	輝	戦
shoot	bottle	shine	war
SHA	BIN	KI	SEN
i*ru*	#	kayaga*ku*	ikusa tataka+
r 41 s 10	r 98 s 11	r 159 s 15	r 62 s 13

1	33
2	34
3	35
4	36
5	37
6	38
7	39
8	40
9	41
10	42
11	43
12	44
13	45
14	46
15	47
16	48
17	49
18	50
19	51
20	52
21	53
22	54
23	55
24	56
25	57
26	58
27	59
28	60
29	61
30	62
31	63
32	64

亻 𡌑 夂 夕

竹	卸	処	外
bamboo	wholesale	deal with	outside; foreign
-	-	-	GAI GE
CHIKU	#	SHO	soto hoka hazu+
take	oroshi oro+	#	r 36 s 5
r 118 s 6	r 26 s 9	r 16* s 5	

免 角

勉	触	解
diligent; strive	touch	unravel; solve
BEN	SHOKU	KAI GE
#	sawa *fu*+	to*ku*..
r 19 s 10	r 148 s 13	r 148 s 13

云 元 尸

魂	頑	所
soul	stubborn	place, site
-	-	
KON	GAN	SHO
tamashii	#	tokoro
r 194 s 14	r 181 s 13	r 63 s 8

豆 鬲 雇

頭	融	顧
head; top	melt, fuse; dissolve	look back
TŌ ZU TO	YŪ	KO
atama kashira	#	kaeri*miru*
r 181 s 16	r 142 s 16	r 181 s 21

丁 干 正 而

頂	刊	政	耐
summit; receive	publish	government	withstand
CHŌ	-	-	-
itadaki itada+	KAN	SEI SHŌ	TAI
r 181 s 11	#	matsurigoto	ta*eru*
	r 18 s 5	r 66 s 9	r 126 s 9

耳 开

敢	刑	形	邪	雅
daring	punishment	shape	wicked	elegant
-	-	-	-	-
KAN	KEI	KEI GYŌ	JA	GA
#	#	katachi kata	#	#
r 66 s 12	r 18 s 6	r 59 s 7	r 163 s 8	r 172 s 13

且 㬎 阝

助	顕	門	即	既
help	obvious	gate, door	immediate; namely; i.e.	already
-	-	-	-	-
JO	KEN	MON	SOKU	KI
suke tasu+	#	kado	#	sude
r 19 s 7	r 181 s 18	r 169 s 8	r 26 s 7	r 71 s 10

里 骨 冊

野	髄	嗣
field; wild	(bone) marrow	heir
YA	ZUI	-
no	#	SHI
r 166 s 11	r 188 s 19	#
		r 30 s 13

原 展

習 弓 君

予 矛 疋

聿 歹 氏

癶 釆

舎 余 分

戋 杀

臨	願	殿		
attend; face	wish, request	Mr, Mrs; palace		
RIN	GAN	DEN TEN		
nozo*mu*	nega*u*	tono -dono		
r 131 s 18	r 181 s 19	r 79 s 13		

改	羽	弱	群	郡
reform	feather, wing	weak	group	county, district
-	-	-	-	-
KAI	U	JAKU	GUN	GUN
arata*meru*..	ha hane	yowa*i*..	mu*re*.. mura	#
r 66 s 7	r 124 s 6	r 57 s 10	r 123 s 13	r 163 s 10

双	預	務	疎	
pair; twin	deposit, entrust	duties	shun; sparse	
-	-	-	-	
SŌ	YO	MU	SO	
futa	azu*keru*..	tsuto*meru*	uto*mu*..	
r 29* s 4	r 181 s 13	r 19 s 11	r 103 s 12	

印	段	卵	邸	
imprint, stamp; sign; India	steps; rank	egg	mansion	
IN	DAN	RAN	TEI	
shirushi	#	tamago	#	
r 26 s 6	r 79 s 9	r 26 s 7	r 163 s 8	

乱	辞	鶏	釈	彩
disorder	word; resign	chicken	explain	color
-	-	-	-	-
RAN	JI	KEI	SHAKU	SAI
mida*su*..	ya*meru*	niwatori	#	irodo*ru*
r 5 s 7	r 160 s 13	r 196 s 19	r 165 s 11	r 59 s 11

領	舗	叙	頒	
territory	shop; pavement	describe	distribute	
-	-	-	-	
RYŌ	HO	JO	HAN	
#	#	#	#	
r 181 s 14	r 9* s 15	r 29* s 9	r 181 s 13	

刈	疑	殺		
reap, mow	doubt	kill		
#	-			
ka*ku*	GI	SATSU SETSU SAI		
	utaga*u*	koro*su*		
r 18 s 4	r 103 s 14	r 79 s 10		

囗 丶 乚 丿 彡

丶

小	心	必	少
small	heart	inevitable	few
-	-	-	-
SHŌ	SHIN	HITSU	SHŌ
chii*sai* ko- o-	kokoro	kanara*zu*	suko*shi* suku+
r 42 s 3	r 61 s 4	r 61 s 5	r 42 s 4

朴	外	掛	赴	以	似
simple	outside; foreign	hang; cost; depend; …	go to	by means of; datum	resemble
-					
BOKU	GAI GE	#	FU	I	JI
#	soto hoka hazu+	kakari ka+	omomu*ku*	#	ni*ru*
r 75 s 6	r 36 s 5	r 64 s 11	r 156 s 9	r 9 s 5	r 9 s 7

秒	抄	妙	砂	劣	省
second (unit of time)	excerpt	miraculous; odd	sand	inferior	minister; omit; reflect upon; …
BYŌ	- SHŌ	- MYŌ	SA SHA	RETSU	SHŌ SEI
#	#	#	suna	oto*ru*	habu*ku* kaeri+
r 115 s 9	r 64 s 7	r 38 s 7	r 112 s 9	r 19 s 6	r 109 s 9

恥	泌	秘	称	跡	嚇
shame; shy	secrete	secret	name, title	vestige, trace, footprints	threaten
CHI	HITSU HI	- HI	- SHŌ	- SEKI	KAKU
haji ha+	#	hi*meru*	#	ato	#
r 61 s 10	r 85 s 8	r 115 s 10	r 115 s 10	r 157 s 13	r 30 s 17

乚

八	入	孤	弧
eight	enter; put in, let in	solitary, orphan	arc, arch
-			
HACHI	NYŪ	KO	KO
ya ya'+ ya+ yō	hai*ru* i+	#	#
r 12 s 2	r 11 s 2	r 39 s 8	r 57 s 9

丿

並	火	秋
line up; ordinary	fire; Tuesday	fall (autumn)
HEI	KA	SHŪ
nara*bu*.. nami	hi ho	aki
r 1* s 8	r 86 s 4	r 115 s 9

彡

形	杉	彩	彰	影
shape	Japanese cedar	color	extol, commend	shadow
-	#	-	SHŌ	EI
KEI GYŌ	sugi	SAI	#	kage
katachi kata	r 75 s 7	irodo*ru*	r 59 s 14	r 59 s 15
r 59 s 7		r 59 s 11		

彫	膨
carve	swell
-	-
CHŌ	BŌ
ho*ru*	fuku*reru*..
r 59 s 11	r 130 s 16

水	永	氷	求	球	承
water; Wednesday	eternal	ice	seek, request	ball	consent; be told
-	-	-	-	-	-
SUI	EI	HYŌ	KYŪ	KYŪ	SHŌ
mizu	naga*i*	kōri kō- hi	moto*meru*	tama	uketamawa*ru*
r 85 s 4	r 85 s 5	r 85 s 5	r 85 s 7	r 96 s 11	r 64 s 8

朴	外	掛	赴		
simple	outside; foreign	hang; cost; depend; …	go to		
-	-	-	-		
BOKU	GAI GE	#	FU		
#	soto hoka hazu+	kakari ka+	omomu*ku*		
r 75 s 6	r 36 s 5	r 64 s 11	r 156 s 9		

非	俳	排	作	昨	詐	酢
un-, non-	*haiku*; actor	repel, expel; anti-	make	yesterday, past	deceive	vinegar
-	-	-		-	-	-
HI	HAI	HAI	SAKU SA	SAKU	SA	SAKU
#	#	#	tsuku*ru*	#	#	su
r 175 s 8	r 9 s 10	r 64 s 11	r 9 s 7	r 72 s 9	r 149 s 12	r 164 s 12

孔	札	礼	乱	乳	沈
hole	chit, tag, banknote	etiquette	disorder	milk; breast	sink (into)
-	-	-	-	-	-
KŌ	SATSU	REI RAI	RAN	NYŪ	CHIN
#	fuda	#	mida*su*..	chichi chi	shizu*mu*..
r 39 s 4	r 75 s 5	r 113 s 5	r 5 s 7	r 5 s 8	r 85 s 7

化	比	北	批	靴	死	尼	泥
transform	compare	north	critique	shoes	death	nun	mud
-	-	-	-	-	-	-	-
KA KE	HI	HOKU	HI	KA	SHI	NI	DEI
ba*keru*..	kura*beru*	kita	#	kutsu	shi*nu*	ama	doro
r 21 s 4	r 81 s 4	r 21 s 5	r 64 s 7	r 177 s 13	r 78 s 6	r 44 s 5	r 85 s 8

兆	挑	桃	跳	眺	逃
sign, omen; trillion	challenge	peach	jump	view, look at	escape
CHŌ	CHŌ	TŌ	CHŌ	CHŌ	TŌ
kiza*shi*..	ido*mu*	momo	to*bu* ha+	naga*meru*	ni*geru*.. noga+
r 10 s 6	r 64 s 9	r 75 s 10	r 157 s 13	r 109 s 11	r 162 s 9

1	33
2	34
3	35
4	36
5	37
6	38
7	39
8	40
9	41
10	42
11	43
12	44
13	45
14	46
15	47
16	48
17	49
18	50
19	51
20	52
21	53
22	54
23	55
24	56
25	57
26	58
27	59
28	60
29	61
30	62
31	63
32	64

丨

引	川	州	訓	酬	肅
pull	river	state, province; sandbank	instruct	reward	solemn; purge
-	-	SHŪ	KŪN	SHU	SHUKU
IN	SEN	su	#	#	#
hiku..	kawa				
r 57 s 4	r 47 s 3	r 47 s 6	r 149 s 10	r 164 s 13	r 129 s 11

刂

刈	刊	刑	判	列	到
reap, mow	publish	punishment	judge	row, line	arrive
#	KAN	KEI	HAN BAN	RETSU	TŌ
kaku	#	#	#	#	#
r 18 s 4	r 18 s 5	r 18 s 6	r 18 s 7	r 18 s 6	r 18 s 8

利	剰	刺	制	則	削
profit, benefit, (loan) interest	surplus	pierce	regulation	rule	whittle; reduce
RI	JŌ	SHI	SEI	SOKU	SAKU
kiku	#	sasu..	#	#	kezuru
r 18 s 7	r 18 s 11	r 18 s 8	r 18 s 8	r 18 , s 9	r 18 s 9

刻	剤	剖	割	別	刷
carve; moment	medicine, drug	dissect	divide up	separate; other; special	print
KOKU	ZAI	BŌ	KATSU	BETSU	SATSU
kizamu	#	#	wari wa+ sa+	wakareru	suru
r 18 s 8	r 18 s 10	r 18 s 10	r 18 s 12	r 18 s 7	r 18 s 8

副	剣	創	剛	劇	
secondary, deputy	sword	create	strong	drama, dramatic	
FUKU	KEN	SŌ	GŌ	GEKI	
#	tsurugi	#	#	#	
r 18 s 11	r 18 s 10	r 18 s 12	r 18 s 10	r 18 s 15	

例	倒	側	測		
example	topple; inverted	side	measure		
REI	TŌ	SOKU	SOKU		
tatoeru	taoreru	kawa	hakaru		
r 9 s 8	r 9 s 10	r 9 s 11	r 85 s 12		

痢	烈	愉			
diarrhea	intense	pleasure			
RI	RETSU	YU			
#	#	#			
r 104 s 12	r 86 s 10	r 61 s 12			

少

抄	秒	妙	砂
excerpt	second (unit of time)	miraculous; odd	sand
SHŌ	BYŌ	MYŌ	SA SHA
#	#	#	suna
r 64 s 7	r 115 s 9	r 38 s 7	r 112 s 9

1	33
2	34
3	35
4	36
5	37
6	38
7	39
8	40
9	41
10	42
11	43
12	44
13	45
14	46
15	47
16	48
17	49
18	50
19	51
20	52
21	53
22	54
23	55
24	56
25	57
26	58
27	59
28	60
29	61
30	62
31	63
32	64

江
inlet, river
KŌ
e
r 85　s 6

紅
crimson
-
KŌ KU
kurenai beni
r 120　s 9

左
left (hand)
SA
hidari
r 48　s 5

佐
assistant
-
SA
#
r 9　s 7

灯
lamp
-
TŌ
hi
r 86　s 6

打
hit
-
DA
u*tsu*
r 64　s 5

訂
revise
-
TEI
#
r 149　s 9

町
town, part of town
CHŌ
machi
r 102　s 7

竹
bamboo
-
CHIKU
take
r 118　s 6

寸
tiny
-
SUN
#
r 41　s 3

可
possible; approve
KA
#
r 30　s 5

河
river
-
KA
kawa
r 85　s 8

何
what, how many
KA
nani nan
r 9　s 7

伺
visit; pay respects
SHI
ukaga*u*
r 9　s 7

幻
illusion
-
GEN
maboroshi
r 52　s 4

行
go; do; line
GYŌ KŌ AN
i*ku* yu+ okona+
r 144　s 6

術
art, skill
-
JUTSU
#
r 60*　s 11

街
street, arcade
GAI KAI
machi
r 60*　s 12

衝
collide
-
SHŌ
#
r 60*　s 15

衛
guard
-
EI
#
r 60*　s 16

衡
balance, scales
KŌ
#
r 60*　s 16

汗
sweat
-
KAN
ase
r 85　s 6

肝
liver
-
KAN
kimo
r 130　s 7

軒
eaves
-
KEN
noki
r 159　s 10

許
permit
-
KYO
yuru*su*
r 149　s 11

坪
tsubo; floor area
#
tsubo
r 32　s 8

評
appraise
-
HYŌ
#
r 149　s 12

呼
call
-
KO
yo*bu*
r 30　s 8

十

汁	針	計
juice, soup	needle	compute; plan
JŪ	- SHIN	KEI
shiru	hari	hakaru..
r 85　s 5	r 167　s 10	r 149　s 9

土

吐	社	圧	在
spit; vomit	company, firm; society; shrine	pressure	be located; exist; suburbs
TO	SHA	- ATSU	ZAI
haku	yashiro	#	aru
r 30　s 6	r 113　s 7	r 32　s 5	r 32　s 6

士

仕	壮
serve	grand, strong
- SHI JI	SŌ
tsukaeru	#
r 9　s 5	r 32*　s 6

生

性	牲	姓
sex; nature, essence	sacrifice	surname
SEI SHŌ	- SEI	SEI SHŌ
#	#	#
r 61　s 8	r 93　s 9	r 38　s 8

朱

株	珠	殊	味	妹
stocks, shares; stump	pearl	special	taste	younger sister
#	- SHU	- SHU	- MI	- MAI
kabu	#	koto	aji aji+	imōto
r 75　s 10	r 96　s 10	r 78　s 10	r 30　s 8	r 38　s 8

失

秩	鉄	銑	洗
order, system	iron	pig iron	wash
CHITSU	- TETSU	SEN	SEN
#	#	#	arau
r 115　s 10	r 167　s 13	r 167　s 14	r 85　s 9

弋 戈 戔

代	弐	式	武		
replace; era; price DAI TAI shiro ka+ yo r 9　s 5	two - NI # r 56*　s 6	rite; style SHIKI # r 154　s 15	military - BU MU # r 77　s 8		
賦	試				
tax; payment FU # r 56　s 6	try - SHI tamesu kokoro+ r 149　s 13				

伐	戦	戯			
cut down - BATSU # r 9　s 6	war - SEN ikusa tataka+ r 62　s 13	play, frolic, jest GI tawamureru r 62　s 15			
我	戒	械	栽	裁	載
I, my; self; selfish GA ware wa r 62　s 7	warn; command KAI imashimeru r 62　s 7	apparatus, machine KAI # r 75　s 11	plant - SAI # r 75　s 10	judge; cut SAI sabaku ta+ r 145　s 12	load; publish SAI noru.. r 159　s 13
域	賊	賦	試		
area, zone IKI # r 32　s 11	robber - ZOKU # r 154　s 13	tax; payment FU # r 154　s 15	try - SHI tamesu kokoro+ r 149　s 13		
繊	織	職	識	餓	機
fine, slender; fiber SEN # r 120　s 17	weave - SHIKI SHOKU oru r 120　s 18	employment - SHOKU # r 128　s 18	discern - SHIKI # r 149　s 19	starve - GA # r 184　s 15	machine, opportunity KI hata r 75　s 16
成	威	滅	減	城	誠
become; consist of SEI JŌ naru.. r 62　s 6	power; threat I # r 38　s 9	perish; destroy METSU horobiru.. r 85　s 13	decrease - GEN heru r 85　s 12	castle - JŌ shiro r 32　s 9	sincerity - SEI makoto r 149　s 13

浅	桟	残	践	銭
shallow - SEN asai r 85　s 9	plank; jetty; bridge SAN # r 75　s 10	remain; cruel ZAN nokosu.. r 78　s 10	carry out, put into practice SEN # r 157　s 13	coin - SEN zeni r 167　s 14

■ 斗 才 寸 犬

斗

料	斜	科
fee; materials	slant	(academic) subject
RYŌ	- SHA	KA
#	nana*me*	#
r 68 s 10	r 68 s 11	r 115 s 9

才

材	財
timber; raw material	finance; property
ZAI	ZAI SAI
#	#
r 75 s 7	r 154 s 10

寸

付	対	村	封	射	討
attach	oppose; pair	village	seal up	shoot	attack
- FU	TAI TSUI	- SON	- FŪ HŌ	- SHA	- TŌ
tsu*ku*..	#	mura	#	i*ru*	u*tsu*
r 9 s 5	r 41 s 7	r 75 s 7	r 41 s 9	r 41 s 10	r 149 s 10

耐	尉	附	樹	謝	慰
withstand	military officer	attach	tree	thank; apology	console, cheer up
- TAI	I	- FU	- JU	SHA	I
ta*eru*	#	#	#	ayama*ru*	nagusa*meru*
r 126 s 9	r 41 s 11	r 170 s 8	r 75 s 16	r 149 s 17	r 61 s 15

犬

伏	状	獣	献	獄
prostrate; ambush	letter; state, condition	beast	offer gift	prison
FUKU	JŌ	- JŪ	KEN KON	- GOKU
fu*u*..	#	kemono	#	#
r 9 s 6	r 94 s 7	r 94 s 16	r 94 s 13	r 94 s 14

就	駄
start to	no good, poor quality
- SHŪ JU	DA
tsu*ku*..	#
r 43 s 12	r 187 s 14

巾 甫 隹 主 羊

帥	師	布	怖
commander	teacher; army	cloth; spread	fear
-			-
SUI	SHI	FU	FU
#	#	nuno	kowai
r 50 s 9	r 50 s 10	r 50 s 5	r 61 s 8

浦	捕	補	舗
bay; shore	catch	compensate; replenish	shop; pavement
HO	HO	HO	HO
ura	toru.. tsuka+	oginau	#
r 85 s 10	r 64 s 10	r 145 s 12	r 9* s 15

准	唯	推	稚	雅	維
quasi-; semi; ratify	only, sole	infer; push, put forward	childish; infant	elegant	fiber; upkeep
JUN	YUI I	SUI	CHI	GA	I
#	#	osu	#	#	#
r 15 s 10	r 30 s 11	r 64 s 11	r 115 s 13	r 172 s 13	r 120 s 14

雄	雑	雌	難	離
male; brave	miscellany	female	difficult	separation
YŪ	ZATSU ZŌ	-	NAN	RI
osu o	#	SHI	katai muzuka+	hanareru..
r 172 s 12	r 172 s 14	mesu me	r 172 s 18	r 172 s 18
		r 172 s 14		

進	確
advance	certainty
-	-
SHIN	KAKU
susumu..	tashika..
r 162 s 11	r 112 s 15

注	住	往	柱	駐
pour; take note	dwell	go; bygone	pillar	reside, stay
CHŪ	JŪ	Ō	CHŪ	CHŪ
sosogu	sumu..	#	hashira	#
r 85 s 8	r 9 s 7	r 60 s 8	r 75 s 9	r 187 s 15

洋	祥	群	詳	鮮
ocean; Western	auspicious	group	detailed	fresh, vivid
YŌ	SHŌ	GUN	SHŌ	SEN
#	#	mure.. mura	kuwashii	azayaka
r 85 s 9	r 113 s 7	r 123 s 13	r 149 s 13	r 195 s 17

1	33
2	34
3	35
4	36
5	37
6	38
7	39
8	40
9	41
10	42
11	43
12	44
13	45
14	46
15	47
16	48
17	49
18	50
19	51
20	52
21	53
22	54
23	55
24	56
25	57
26	58
27	59
28	60
29	61
30	62
31	63
32	64

力 刀 勹

力

功	幼	助	効	劾	勅
merit; achievement	infant	help	effective	denounce, impeach	imperial edict
-	-	-	-	-	-
KŌ KU	YŌ	JO	KŌ	GAI	CHOKU
#	osana*i*	suke tasu+	ki*ku*	#	#
r 19 s 5	r 52 s 5	r 19 s 7	r 19 s 8	r 19 s 8	r 19 s 9

励	動	勤	勘	勧	働
encourage; diligent	move	work hard, serve	intuition; consider	advise; encourage	work
REI	-	KIN GON	KAN	KAN	-
hage*mu*..	DŌ	tsuto*meru*	#	susu*meru*	DŌ
r 19 s 7	ugo*ku*..	r 19 s 12	r 19 s 11	r 19 s 13	hatara*ku*
	r 19 s 11				r 9 s 13

勉	協
diligent; strive	co-operate
-	-
BEN	KYŌ
#	#
r 19 s 10	r 24 s 8

刀

切	初
cut	first time
-	-
SETSU SAI	SHO
ki*ru*..	hatsu- ui- haji+ -so+
r 18 s 4	r 18 s 7

幻	辺	喫
illusion	vicinity	eat, drink, smoke
-	-	-
GEN	HEN	KITSU
maboroshi	ata*ri* -be	#
r 52 s 4	r 162 s 5	r 30 s 12

勹

的	酌	約	釣	均
target; -like	serve wine	pledge; approx.	fishing; hanging	equal
TEKI	-	YAKU	CHŌ	-
mato	SHAKU	#	tsu*ru*	KIN
r 106 s 8	#	r 120 s 9	r 167 s 11	#
	r 164 s 10			r 32 s 7

立
文
交
亢
方

泣	位	粒
weep, cry	rank; approx.	particle, grain of
KYŪ	I	RYŪ
na*ku*	kurai	tsubu
r 85　s 8	r 9　s 7	r 119　s 11

蚊	紋
mosquito	family crest
-	MON
ka	#
r 142　s 10	r 120　s 10

校	較	絞
school	compare	strangle
-	-	-
KŌ	KAKU	KŌ
#	#	shibo*ru* shi+
r 75　s 10	r 159　s 13	r 120　s 12

坑	抗	航
pit	oppose	navigate
-	-	-
KŌ	KŌ	KŌ
#	#	#
r 32　s 7	r 64　s 7	r 137　s 10

坊	妨	防	肪	紡
boy; priest	obstruct	prevent	animal fat	spin (yarn)
BŌ BO'	-	-	-	-
#	BŌ	BŌ	BŌ	BŌ
	samata*geru*	fuse*gu*	#	tsumu*gu*
r 32　s 7	r 38　s 7	r 170　s 7	r 130　s 8	r 120　s 10

訪
visit
-
HŌ
tazu*neru* otozu+
r 149　s 11

1	33
2	34
3	35
4	36
5	37
6	38
7	39
8	40
9	41
10	42
11	43
12	44
13	45
14	46
15	47
16	48
17	49
18	50
19	51
20	52
21	53
22	54
23	55
24	56
25	57
26	58
27	59
28	60
29	61
30	62
31	63
32	64

欠 夂

欠

次 next - JI SHI tsugi tsu+ r76 s6	炊 cook, boil SUI taku r86 s8	吹 blow - SUI fuku r30 s7	欧 Europe - Ō # r76 s8	軟 soft - NAN yawaraka.. r159 s11	欺 deceive, cheat GI azamuku r76 s12
欲 desire - YOKU hossuru ho+ r76 s11	飲 drink - IN nomu r184 s12	款 clause; cordial KAN # r76 s12	歓 delight - KAN # r76 s15	歌 song, sing KA uta uta+ r76 s14	
畝 ridge se # une se r102 s10	称 name, title - SHŌ # r115 s10				

夂

攻 assault - KŌ semeru r66 s7	改 reform - KAI aratameru.. r66 s7	枚 sheet (of paper) MAI # r75 s8	牧 pasture - BOKU maki r93 s8	政 government - SEI SHŌ matsurigoto r66 s9	放 set free; emit HŌ hanatsu.. r66 s8
救 rescue - KYŪ sukuu r66 s11v	敗 be defeated HAI yabureru r66 s11	敢 daring - KAN # r66 s12	敏 agile, alert BIN # r66 s10	故 old; dead; intent KO yue r66 s9	致 cause; do CHI itasu r133 s10
赦 pardon, forgive SHA # r155 s11	教 teach - KYŌ oshieru oso+ r66 s11	散 scatter - SAN chiru.. r66 s12	敬 respect - KEI uyamau r66 s12		
数 number - SŪ SU kazu kazo+ r66 s13	敵 enemy - TEKI kataki r66 s15	敷 spread - FU shiku r66 s15			
倣 imitate - HŌ narau r9 s10	徴 symptom; levy CHŌ # r60 s14	微 tiny, faint, hard to see BI # r60 s13	徹 thorough - TETSU # r60 s15	撤 withdraw - TETSU # r64 s15	激 violent - GEKI hageshii r85 s16

又 反 皮 及

双	収	奴	叙	取	叔
pair; twin	obtain; seize; collect; …	slave; guy	describe	take	aunt, uncle
-	-	-	-	-	-
SŌ	SHŪ	DO NU	JO	SHU	SHUKU
futa	osameru..	#	#	toru	#
r 29* s 4	r 29* s 5	r 38 s 5	r 29* s 9	r 29 s 8	r 29 s 8

淑	友	服	報	極	趣
graceful	friend	clothes; obey	report; reward	extremes	gist; motive; elegance
-	-	-	-		
SHUKU	YŪ	FUKU	HŌ	KYOKU GOKU	SHŪ
#	tomo	#	mukuiru	kiwami..	omomuki
r 85 s 11	r 29 s 4	r 130* s 8	r 32 s 12	r 75 s 12	r 156 s 15

仮	坂	板	版	販	飯
temporary	slope	board	printing	sell, trade	meal, cooked rice
-					
KA KE	HAN	HAN BAN	HAN	HAN	HAN
kari	saka	ita	#	#	meshi
r 9 s 6	r 32 s 7	r 75 s 8	r 91 s 8	r 154 s 11	r 184 s 12

返
return, repay
HEN
kaeru..
r 162 s 7

波	披	彼	破	被
waves	announce	he, she, they; that (yonder)	break, ruin	undergo, -ee; wear, cover
-	-	-	-	-
HA	HI	HI	HA	HI
nami	#	kare kano	yaburu..	kōmoru
r 85 s 8	r 64 s 8	r 60 s 8	r 112 s 10	r 145 s 0

吸	扱	級
suck, inhale	deal with	grade, rank
-	-	-
KYŪ	#	KYŪ
suu	atsukau	#
r 30 s 6	r 64 s 6	r 120 s 9

█▌ 己 包 也 屯

己

妃	記	紀	配	起
queen, empress	write down	era; chronicle	distribute	wake up, rise; begin
HI	KI	KI	HAI	KI
#	shiru*su*	#	kuba*ru*	o*kiru*..
r 38 s 6	r 149 s 10	r 120 s 9	r 164 s 10	r 156 s 10

包

泡	胞	砲	飽	抱
bubbles	placenta	cannon	sated	embrace
-	-	-	-	-
HŌ	HŌ	HŌ	HŌ	HŌ
awa	#	#	a*kiru*.. ヽ	da*ku* ida+ kaka+
r 85 s 8	r 130 s 9	r 112 s 10	r 184 s 13	r 64 s 8

也

池	他	地		
pond	other	earth, ground; place		
CHI	TA	CHI JI		
ike	#	#		
r 85 s 6	r 9 s 5	r 32 s 6		

屯

純	鈍			
pure	dull, slow			
-	-			
JUN	DON			
#	nibu*i*			
r 120 s 10	r 167 s 12			

■ 几 斤 兂

机	肌	飢
desk	skin	hunger, starve
-	#	KI
KI	hada	ueru
tsukue	r 130 s 6	r 184 s 10
r 75 s 6		

帆	処	拠
sail	deal with	basis
-	-	-
HAN	SHO	KYO KO
ho	#	#
r 50 s 6	r 16* s 5	r 64 s 8

折	析	祈	所	新
fold, snap; occasion	analyze	pray	place, site	new
SETSU	SEKI	-	SHO	-
ori o+	#	KI	tokoro	SHIN
r 64 s 7	r 75 s 8	inoru	r 63 s 8	nii- atara+ ara+
		r 113 s 7		r 69 s 13

断	漸	近	匠	逝	訴
sever; decide	gradually	near; recent	craftsman	die, death	sue; appeal
DAN	ZEN	-	-	-	SO
kotowaru ta+	#	KIN	SHŌ	SEI	uttaeru
r 69 s 11	r 85 s 14	chikai	#	yuku	r 149 s 12
		r 162 s 7	r 22 s 6	r 162 s 10	

既	慨	概
already	deplore	in general; roughly
-	-	-
KI	GAI	GAI
sude	#	#
r 71 s 10	r 61 s 13	r 75 s 14

■ 口 田 由 申 甲

加 add; join in KA kuwa*eru*.. r 19 s 5	**如** as, like, such as JO NYO # r 38 s 6	**知** know - CHI shi*ru* r 111 s 8	**和** harmony; Japan WA O nago*mu*.. yawa+ r 30 s 8

口

畑 field - # hata hatake r 102 s 9	**細** thin, fine SAI hoso*i*.. koma+ r 120 s 11

田

油 oil - YU abura r 85 s 8	**抽** draw out, extract CHŪ # r 64 s 8	**軸** axle, axis JIKU # r 159 s 12

由

伸 extend, stretch SHIN no*biru*.. r 9 s 7	**神** god - SHIN JIN kami kan- kō r 113 s 7	**紳** gentleman - SHIN # r 120 s 11	**沖** open sea - CHŪ oki r 85 s 7	**仲** relationship - CHŪ naka r 9 s 6

申

押 push - Ō o*su*.. r 64 s 8	**岬** headland, cape # misaki r 46 s 8

甲

泊	伯	拍	舶	旧
overnight	aunt, uncle; earl	clap; beat, tempo	large ship	old, former
-	-	-	-	-
HAKU	HAKU	HAKU HYŌ	HAKU	KYŪ
to*maru*..	#	#	#	#
r 85　s 8	r 9　s 7	r 64　s 8	r 137　s 11	r 72*　s 5

阻	祖	租	粗	組	相
obstruct	ancestor	tax, tribute, levy	coarse	group, union	mutual; minister
-	-	-	-	-	-
SO	SO	SO	SO	SO	SŌ SHŌ
haba*mu*	#	#	ara*i*	kumi ku+	ai-
r 170　s 8	r 113　s 7	r 115　s 10	r 119　s 11	r 120　s 11	r 109　s 9

規	視	現	親	観
regulation	look at, watch	present, visible, existing, actual	parent, kin; intimate	view; observe
KI	SHI	GEN	SHIN	KAN
#	#	arawa*reru*..	oya shita+	#
r 147　s 11	r 147　s 11	r 96　s 11	r 147　s 16	r 147　s 18

頂	項	煩	頼
summit; receive	clause	trouble, worry	rely on; request
CHŌ	KŌ	HAN BON	RAI
itadaki itada+	#	wazura*u*..	tayo*ru* tano+
r 181　s 11	r 181　s 12	r 86　s 13	r 181*　s 16

頒	領	額	頻	類
distribute	territory	sum; frame; forehead	frequent	sort, kind
-	-	-	-	-
HAN	RYŌ	GAKU	HIN	RUI
#	#	hitai	#	#
r 181　s 13	r 181　s 14	r 181　s 18	r 181　s 17	r 181　s 18

頑	預	頭	顕
stubborn	deposit, entrust	head; top	obvious
-	-	TŌ ZU TO	-
GAN	YO	atama kashira	KEN
#	azu*keru*..		#
r 181　s 13	r 181　s 13	r 181　s 16	r 181　s 18

順	傾	瀬
sequence; obey	inclination	shallows, rapids
JUN	-	#
#	KEI	se
r 181　s 12	katamu*ku*..	r 85　s 19
	r 9　s 13	

顔	願	顧	題
face	wish, request	look back	title, topic
-	-	-	-
GAN	GAN	KO	DAI
kao	nega*u*	kaeri*miru*	#
r 181　s 18	r 181　s 19	r 181　s 21	r 181　s 18

▉ 卩 阝 尺 月

卩

印	却	即	卸	犯	卵
imprint, stamp; sign; India	reject; exclude	immediate; namely; i.e.	wholesale	crime	egg
IN	KYAKU	SOKU	-	HAN	RAN
shirushi	#	#	oroshi oro+	oka*su*	tamago
r 26 s 6	r 26 s 7	r 26 s 7	r 26 s 9	r 94 s 5	r 26 s 7

仰	抑	柳	脚	御	迎
look up at; respect	restrain, suppress	willow	leg, foot	(honorific); control	welcome
GYŌ KŌ	YOKU	RYŪ	KYAKU KYA	GYO GO	GEI
ao*gu* ō+	osa*eru*	yanagi	ashi	on-	muka*eru*
r 9 s 6	r 64 s 7	r 75 s 9	r 130 s 11	r 60 s 12	r 162 s 7

阝

邦	邪	郡	郎	郊	邸
homeland; Japan	wicked	county, district	man	outskirts, suburbs	mansion
HŌ	JA	GUN	RŌ	KŌ	TEI
#	#	#	#	#	#
r 163 s 7	r 163 s 8	r 163 s 10	r 163 s 9	r 163 s 9	r 163 s 8

部	郭	都	郵	郷	廊
section	enclosure	city, capital	mail	hometown; rural	corridor
-	KAKU	TO TSU	YŪ	KYŌ GŌ	RŌ
BU	#	miyako	#	#	#
#					
r 163 s 11	r 163 s 11	r 163 s 11	r 163 s 11	r 163 s 11	r 53 s 12

尺

沢	択	訳	釈	駅
marsh; plenty; ...	choose	translate	explain	station
TAKU	TAKU	YAKU	SHAKU	EKI
sawa	#	wake	#	#
r 85 s 7	r 64 s 7	r 149 s 11	r 165 s 11	r 187 s 14

月

明	朗	朝	期
bright; next	cheerful; bright, clear	morning; dynasty	term; expect
MYŌ MEI	RŌ	CHŌ	KI
a*ku*.. aki+ aka+	hoga*raka*	asa	#
r 72 s 8	r 130* s 10	r 130* s 12	r 130* s 12

湖	潮	棚
lake	tide; seawater	shelf
-	CHŌ	-
KO	shio	#
mizuumi		tana
r 85 s 12	r 85 s 15	r 75 s 12

有	賄	随	髄	門
have; exist	bribe; pay for	follow	(bone) marrow	gate, door
YŪ U	WAI	ZUI	ZUI	MON
a*ru*	makana*u*	#	#	kado
r 130* s 6	r 154 s 13	r 170 s 12	r 188 s 19	r 169 s 8

服	報	眠
clothes; obey	report; reward	sleep
FUKU	HŌ	-
#	muku*iru*..	MIN
r 130* s 8	r 32 s 12	nemu*ru*..
		r 109 s 10

恨	根	限	眼	銀
grudge; regret	root	limit	eye	silver
KON	KON	GEN	GAN GEN	GIN
ura*mu*..	ne	kagi*ru*	manako	#
r 61 s 9	r 75 s 10	r 170 s 9	r 109 s 11	r 167 s 14

退	眠
retreat	sleep
-	-
TAI	MIN
shirizo*ku*..	nemu*ru*..
r 162 s 9	r 109 s 10

浪	娘
waves; roam	daughter
RŌ	-
#	#
r 85 s 10	musume
	r 38 s 10

伺	詞	飼	嗣
visit; pay respects	word	raise, breed	heir
SHI	SHI	SHI	SHI
ukaga*u*	#	ka*u*	#
r 9 s 7	r 149 s 12	r 184 s 13	r 30 s 13

■ ム 区 乍 長

ム	仏 Buddha; France BUTSU hotoke r 9　s 4	払 pay; clear away FUTSU hara*u* r 64　s 5	私 I; private - SHI watakushi r 115　s 7		
区	枢 pivotal - SŪ # r 75　s 8	駆 spur on; drive; expel KU ka*ru*.. r 187　s 14			
乍	作 make - SAKU SA tsuku*ru* r 9　s 7	昨 yesterday, past SAKU # r 72　s 9	酢 vinegar - SAKU su r 164　s 12	詐 deceive - SA # r 149　s 12	許 permit - KYO yuru*su* r 149　s 11
長	張 stretch - CHŌ ha*ru* r 57　s 11	帳 notebook; curtain CHŌ # r 50　s 11	脹 expand - CHŌ # r 130　s 12		

独
alone;
Germany
DOKU
hito*ri*
r 94　s 9

触
touch
-
SHOKU
sawa *fu*+
r 148　s 13

融
melt, fuse;
dissolve
YŪ
#
r 142　s 16

沖
open sea
-
CHŪ
oki
r 85　s 7

仲
relationship
-
CHŪ
naka
r 9　s 6

鳴
(animal) cry,
howl; sound
MEI
na*ku*..
r 196　s 14

鶏
chicken
-
KEI
niwatori
r 196　s 19

塊
lump
-
KAI
katamari
r 32　s 13

魂
soul
-
KON
tamashii
r 194　s 14

醜
ugly
-
SHŪ
miniku*i*
r 164　s 17

殳

没	役	投	殴	段	般
sink; die; disappear	service, duty	throw; send in	assault -	steps; rank	sort, kind; time
BOTSU	EKI YAKU	TŌ	Ō	DAN	HAN
#	#	nageru	naguru	#	#
r 85　s 7	r 60　s 7	r 64　s 7	r 79　s 8	r 79　s 9	r 137　s 10

設	殻	穀	殺
establish -	shell -	grain, cereal	kill
SETSU	KAKU	KOKU	SATSU SETSU SAI
mōkeru	kara	#	korosu
r 149　s 11	r 79　s 11	r 115　s 14	r 79　s 10

搬	鍛	殿
convey -	forge metal; training	Mr, Mrs; palace
HAN	TAN	DEN TEN
#	kitaeru	tono -dono
r 64　s 13	r 167　s 17	r 79　s 13

支

技	枝	岐	肢	鼓
skill	branch -	diverge	limb -	drum
GI	SHI	KI	SHI	KO
waza	eda	#	#	tsuzumi
r 64　s 7	r 75　s 8	r 46　s 7	r 130　s 8	r 207　s 13

圣

径	怪	軽	経
path; diameter	strange, weird, spooky	light, slight	pass through; economics; …
KEI	KAI	KEI	KEI KYŌ
#	ayashii..	karui karo+	heru
r 60　s 8	r 61　s 8	r 159　s 12	r 120　s 11

卆

枠	粋	砕	酔
frame -	pure, elegant	pulverize -	drunk -
#	SUI	SAI	SUI
waku	#	kudakeru..	you
r 75　s 8	r 119　s 10	r 112　s 9	r 164　s 11

■◨ 分 令 僉 青 寺

粉	紛				
flour, powder	confuse				
FUN	- FUN				
kona ko	magi*reru*..				
r 119 s 10	r 120 s 10				

鈴	齢	冷			
bell	age	cold			
- REI RIN	- REI	- REI			
suzu		tsume*tai* hi+ sa+			
r 167 s 13	r 211 s 17	r 15 s 7			

倹	検	険	験		
thrifty	examine	steep; risk	examine; effect		
- KEN	- KEN	KEN	KEN GEN		
#	#	kewa*shii*	#		
r 9 s 10	r 75 s 12	r 170 s 11	r 187 s 18		

精	晴	請	清	漬	債
spirit, essence	fine weather	request	pure	pickle	debt
SEI SHŌ	SEI	SEI SHIN	SEI SHŌ	-	SAI
#	ha*reru*..	ko*u* u+	kiyo*i*..	# tsu*keru*..	#
r 119 s 14	r 72 s 12	r 149 s 15	r 85 s 11	r 85 s 14	r 9 s 13

侍	待	持	特	時	詩
samurai; serve	await	hold, have	special	time; hour	poem
JI	- TAI	JI	- TOKU	JI	SHI
samurai	ma*tsu*	mo*tsu*	#	toki	#
r 9 s 8	r 60 s 9	r 64 s 9	r 93 s 10	r 72 s 10	r 149 s 13

㕣

谷

台

各

舌

沿	船	鉛			
along	ship	lead			
-	-	(the metal)			
EN	SEN	EN			
so*u*	fune funa-	namari			
r 85　s 8	r 137　s 11	r 167　s 13			

浴	俗	裕	給	拾	捨
bathe	vulgar;	abundant	supply,	pick up,	discard
-	custom	-	pay	acquire	-
YOKU	ZOKU	YŪ	KYŪ	SHŪ JU	SHA
a*biru..*	#	#	#	hiro*u*	su*teru*
r 85　s 10	r 9　s 9	r 145　s 12	r 120　s 12	r 64　s 9	r 64　s 11

治	始	胎			
govern;	begin	womb			
heal	-	-			
JI CHI	SHI	TAI			
nao*ru..* osa+	haji*maru..*	#			
r 85　s 8	r 38　s 8	r 130　s 9			

格	略	路	酪	絡	銘
state,	abbreviate	road,	dairy	entwine;	inscription
condition		way	produce	link	-
KAKU KŌ	RYAKU	RO	RAKU	RAKU	MEI
#	#	-ji	#	kara*mu..*	#
r 75　s 10	r 102　s 11	r 157　s 13	r 164　s 13	r 120　s 12	r 167　s 14

活	括	話	粘		
active	fastern; lump	speak;	sticky		
-	together	tale	-		
KATSU	KATSU	WA	NEN		
#	#	hanashi hana+	neba*ru*		
r 85　s 9	r 64　s 9	r 149　s 13	r 119　s 11		

■ 召 兌

沼	招	昭	詔	紹
marsh	invite	clear, bright	imperial edict	introduce
-	-	-	-	-
SHŌ	SHŌ	SHŌ	SHŌ	SHŌ
numa	mane*ku*	#	mikotonori	#
r 85 s 8	r 64 s 8	r 72 s 9	r 149 s 12	r 120 s 11

悦	税	脱	説	鋭
joy	tax	remove; escape	explanation	sharp
-	-	DATSU	-	EI
ETSU	ZEI	nu*gu*..	SETSU ZEI	surudo*i*
#	#		to*ku*	
r 61 s 10	r 115 s 12	r 130 s 11	r 149 s 14	r 167 s 15

況	祝
conditions	celebrate
-	-
KYŌ	SHUKU SHŪ
#	iwa*u*
r 85 s 8	r 113 s 7

方 辛 京 竞
広 東 隶
止 本 未
占 中
先 告
关 半
匕
丩 甘 井

訪	辞	涼	鯨	競
visit	word; resign	cool	whale	compete
-	-	-	-	-
HŌ	JI	RYŌ	GEI	KYŌ KEI
tazu*neru* otozu+	ya*meru*	suzu*shii*..	kujira	kiso*u* se+
r 149 s 11	r 160 s 13	r 85 s 11	r 195 s 19	r 117 s 20

鉱	疎	隷		
ore, mine	shun; sparse	servant, subordinate		
KŌ	SO	REI		
#	uto*mu*..	#		
r 167 s 13	r 103 s 12	r 171 s 16		

祉	鉢	味	妹	
welfare	bowl, pot	taste	younger sister	
-	-	-	-	
SHI	HACHI HATSU	MI	MAI	
#	#	aji aji+	imōto	
r 113 s 7	r 167 s 13	r 30 s 8	r 38 s 8	

粘	仲	沖		
sticky	relationship	open sea		
-	-	-		
NEN	CHU	CHU		
neba*ru*	naka	oki		
r 119 s 11	r 9 s 6	r 85 s 7		

洗	銑	酷		
wash	pig iron	severe		
-	-	-		
SEN	SEN	KOKU		
ara*u*	#	#		
r 85 s 9	r 167 s 14	r 164 s 14		

咲	朕	畔		
bloom	I, we (imperial)	shore		
-	-	-		
#	CHIN	HAN		
sa*ku*	#	#		
r 30 s 9	r 74 s 10	r 102 s 10		

能				
ability; *Noh* play				
NŌ				
#				
r 130 s 10				

叫	紺	耕	併	
shout	dark blue	plow	combine, unite	
-	-	-	HEI	
KYŌ	KON	KŌ	awa*seru*	
sake*bu*	#	tagaya*su*	r 9 s 8	
r 30 s 6	r 120 s 11	r 127 s 10		

以 太 火

似 丸 尤 内

丁 午 尔 布

争 勿 久

亡 名

以	似	駄	秋
by means of; datum	resemble	no good, poor quality	fall (autumn)
I	JI	DA	SHŪ
#	ni*ru*	#	aki
r 9 s 5	r 9 s 7	r 187 s 14	r 115 s 9
軌	執	就	納
track, orbit	grasp; carry out	start to	pay; obtain; store; supply
KI	SHITSU SHŪ	SHŪ JU	NŌ NA NA' NAN TO
#	to*ru*	tsu*ku..*	osa*meru..*
r 159 s 9	r 32 s 11	r 43 s 12	r 120 s 10
竹	許	称	飾
bamboo	permit	name, title	decorate
CHIKU	KYO	SHŌ	SHOKU
take	yuru*su*	#	kaza*ru*
r 118 s 6	r 149 s 11	r 115 s 10	r 184 s 13
浄	静	物	畝
pure	quiet	thing	ridge
JŌ	SEI JŌ	BUTSU MOTSU	*se*
#	shizu shizu+	mono	une se
r 85 s 9	r 174 s 14	r 93 s 8	r 102 s 10
乾	銘		
dry	inscription		
KAN	MEI		
kawa*ku..*	#		
r 5 s 11	r 167 s 14		

1	33
2	34
3	35
4	36
5	37
6	38
7	39
8	40
9	41
10	42
11	43
12	44
13	45
14	46
15	47
16	48
17	49
18	50
19	51
20	52
21	53
22	54
23	55
24	56
25	57
26	58
27	59
28	60
29	61
30	62
31	63
32	64

丂 帀 瓦

王 正

不 开

云 尸 巨

卩 巳 予 翠

丁 彐 弓 子

巧	朽	師	瓶
skillful	decay	teacher; army	bottle
-	-	-	-
KŌ	KYŪ	SHI	BIN
takumi	kuchiru	#	#
r 48 s 5	r 75 s 6	r 50 s 10	r 98 s 11
狂	班	征	証
mad	squad	conquer; go to war	proof, evidence
-	-	-	-
KYŌ	HAN	SEI	SHŌ
kuruu..	#	#	#
r 94 s 7	r 96 s 10	r 60 s 8	r 149 s 12
杯	研	併	
cup, glass	hone, grind, polish	combine, unite	
HAI	KEN	HEI	
sakazuki	togu	awaseru	
r 75 s 8	r 112 s 9	r 9 s 8	

伝	転	炉	拒	距
transmit	revolve; overturn	furnace, hearth	reject	distance
-	-	-	-	-
DEN	TEN	RO	KYO	KYO
tsutaeru..	korobu..	#	#	kobamu
r 9 s 6	r 159 s 11	r 86 s 8	r 157 s 12	r 64 s 8
卵	犯	野	解	
egg	crime	field; wild	unravel; solve	
-	-	-	-	
RAN	HAN	YA	KAI GE	
tamago	okasu	no	toku..	
r 26 s 7	r 94 s 5	r 166 s 11	r 148 s 13	
幻	羽	翻	弱	好
illusion	feather, wing	flip; translate	weak	good; fond of
-	-	-	-	-
GEN	U	HON	JAKU	KŌ
maboroshi	ha hane	hirugaesu..	yowai..	konomu su+
r 52 s 4	r 124 s 6	r 124 s 18	r 57 s 10	r 38 s 6

■

旧	相	門	潤	欄
old, former	mutual; minister	gate, door	moisten	railing; column (in newspaper)
KYŪ	SŌ SHŌ	MON	- JUN	RAN
#	ai-	kado	uruou.. uru+	#
r 72* s 5	r 109 s 9	r 169 s 8	r 85 s 15	r 75 s 20

況	祝	損	韻	絹
conditions	celebrate	loss, harm; fail to	rhyme, tone	silk
- KYŌ	- SHUKU SHŪ	SON	IN	- KEN
#	iwau	sokonau..	#	kinu
r 85 s 8	r 113 s 7	r 64 s 13	r 180 s 19	r 120 s 13

絵	幹	蛇
picture	trunk, main part	snake
- E KAI	KAN	JA DA
#	miki	hebi
r 120 s 12	r 51 s 13	r 142 s 11

託	耗	任	妊
entrust	use up, wear out	entrust; duties	pregnant
- TAKU	MŌ KŌ	NIN	- NIN
#	#	makaseru..	#
r 149 s 10	r 127 s 10	r 9 s 6	r 38 s 7

訴	紙
sue; appeal	paper
SO	- SHI
uttaeru	kami
r 149 s 12	r 120 s 10

丶 ノ

丶

主 master - SHU SU nushi omo r 3 s 5	心 heart - SHIN kokoro r 61 s 4	永 eternal - EI naga*i* r 85 s 5	必 inevitable - HITSU kanara*zu* r 61 s 5	求 seek, request KYŪ moto*meru* r 85 s 7	氷 ice - HYŌ kōri kō- hi r 85 s 5
犬 dog - KEN inu r 94 s 4	式 rite; style SHIKI # r 56 s 6	弍 two - NI # r 56* s 6	武 military - BU MU # r 77 s 8	戒 warn; command KAI imashi*meru* r 62 s 7	我 I, my; self; selfish GA ware wa r 62 s 7
成 become; consist of SEI JŌ na*ru*.. r 62 s 6	威 power; threat I # r 38 s 9	栽 plant - SAI # r 75 s 10	載 load; publish SAI no*ru*.. r 159 s 13	裁 judge; cut SAI saba*ku* ta+ r 145 s 12	
注 pour; note CHŪ soso*gu* r 85 s 8	泳 swim - EI oyo*gu* r 85 s 8	述 say - JUTSU no*beru* r 162 s 8	為 do; purpose I # r 86* s 9		

ノ

血 blood - KETSU chi r 143 s 6	向 facing - KŌ mu*kau*.. r 30 s 6	舟 boat - SHŪ fune funa- r 137 s 6	自 oneself - JI SHI mizuka*ra* r 132 s 6	白 white - HAKU BYAKU shiro*i* shiro shira- r 106 s 5	
良 good - RYŌ yoi r 138 s 7	皇 emperor - Ō KŌ # r 106 s 9	泉 spring; spa SEN izumi r 85 s 9	卑 lowly - HI iya*shii*.. r 24 s 9	鬼 demon; ghost KI oni r 194 s 10	
身 body; self SHIN mi r 158 s 7	鳥 bird - CHŌ tori r 196 s 11	島 island - TŌ shima r 46 s 10	息 stinking - SHŪ kusa*i* r 132 s 9	臭 breath; child SOKU iki r 61 s 10	鼻 nose - BI hana r 209 s 14
衆 the people - SHŪ SHU # r 143 s 12	奥 inmost, core Ō oku r 37 s 12	楽 music; joy GAKU RAKU tano*shii*.. r 75 s 13	迫 press, urge; approach HAKU sema*ru* r 162 s 8	追 chase; expel TSUI *ou* r 162 s 9	

羊	弟	兼
sheep	younger brother	combined; unable
-	TEI DAI DE	KEN
YŌ	otōto	ka*neru*
hitsuji	r 57 s 7	r 12 s 10
r 123 s 6		

半	米	券	巻
half, semi-, pen-	rice; America	ticket	roll; scroll; book
HAN	BEI MAI	-	KAN
naka*ba*	kome	KEN	maki ma+
r 24 s 5	r 119 s 6	# r 18 s 8	r 49* s 9

並	益	首	前	普	慈
line up; ordinary	benefit	head, neck; chief	before	universal	compassion
HEI	-	SHU	-	FU	JI
nara*bu.. *nami	EKI YAKU	kubi	ZEN	#	itsuku*shimu*
r 1* s 8	# r 108 s 10	r 185 s 9	mae	r 72 s 12	r 61 s 13
			r 18 s 9		

羊	弟	兼
sheep	younger brother	combined; unable
-	TEI DAI DE	KEN
YŌ	otōto	ka*neru*
hitsuji	r 57 s 7	r 12 s 10
r 123 s 6		

送	逆	遂	道	遵	導
send	inverse; counter-	accomplish	way, road	comply	guide
-	GYAKU	-	DŌ TŌ	JUN	DŌ
SŌ	saka saka+	SUI	michi	#	michibi*ku*
oku*ru*	r 162 s 9	to*geru*	r 162 s 12	r 162 s 15	r 41 s 15
r 162 s 9		r 162 s 12			

羊	差	着	善
sheep	difference	arrive; wear, clothes	good
-	-	CHAKU JAKU	ZEN
YŌ	SA	ki*ru.. *tsu+	yo*i*
hitsuji	sa*su*	r 109* s 12	r 30 s 12
r 123 s 6	r 48 s 10		

美	養	義
beauty	foster, rear	righteous; meaning; ...
-	YŌ	GI
BI	yashina*u*	#
utsuku*shii*	r 184 s 15	r 123 s 13
r 123 s 9		

八 八 人 小

父 father - FU chichi r 88 s 4	**谷** valley - KOKU tani r 150 s 7			
公 public; official KŌ ōyake r 12 s 4	**分** portion; minutes BU FUN BUN wakeru.. r 18 s 4	**盆** tray - BON # r 108 s 9	**貧** poverty - HIN BIN mazushii r 154 s 11	**翁** old man - Ō # r 124 s 10
今 now KIN KON ima r 9 s 4	**合** unite; agree; fit GŌ GA' KA' au.. r 30 s 6	**会** meet KAI E au r 9* s 6	**令** orders - REI # r 9 s 5	**命** fate; life; orders MYŌ MEI inochi r 30 s 8
介 mediate KAI # r 9 s 4	**企** plan - KI kuwadateru r 9 s 6	**全** whole - ZEN mattaku r 9* s 6	**余** remainder; surplus YO amaru.. r 9 s 7	**金** money; metal; gold; Friday KIN KON kane kana- r 167 s 8
舎 building, house, hut SHA # r 9* s 8	**含** include, contain GAN fukumu.. r 30 s 7	**念** thought; desire NEN # r 61 s 9		
倉 warehouse - SŌ kura r 9 s 10	**食** eat, food SHOKU JIKI taberu ku+ r 184 s 9	**傘** umbrella - SAN kasa r 9 s 12	**途** way - TO # r 162 s 10	
少 few - SHŌ sukoshi suku+ r 42 s 4	**劣** inferior - RETSU otoru r 19 s 6	**省** minister; omit; reflect upon; ... SHŌ SEI habuku kaeri+ r 109 s 9		

単	巣	挙	誉	厳
single, simple	nest	raise; arrest; whole; …	honor	severe
TAN	- SŌ	KYO	- YO	GEN GON
#	su	*ageru*..	homa*re*	kibi*shii* ogoso+
r 24* s 9	r 75* s 11	r 64 s 10	r 149 s 13	r 27* s 17

挙	誉	単	巣	厳
raise; arrest; whole; …	honor	single, simple	nest	severe
KYO	- YO	TAN	- SŌ	GEN GON
ageru..	homa*re*	#	su	kibi*shii* ogoso+
r 64 s 10	r 149 s 13	r 24* s 9	r 75* s 11	r 27* s 17

労	栄	学	蛍	営	覚
labor	glory; prosper	study, learning	firefly	management	memorize; awake
- RŌ	EI	GAKU	- KEI	- EI	KAKU
#	hae.. saka+	mana*bu*	hotaru	itona*mu*	obo*eru* sa+
r 19 s 7	r 75 s 9	r 39 s 8	r 142 s 11	r 30* s 12	r 147 s 12

光	当	肖	尚		
light	hit; this; applicable	resemble	respect; valued		
- KŌ	TŌ	SHŌ	SHŌ		
hikari hika+	a*teru*..	#	#		
r 10 s 6	r 58* s 6	r 130 s 7	r 42 s 8		

半	米	券	巻		
half, semi-, pen-	rice; America	ticket	roll; scroll; book		
HAN	BEI MAI	- KEN	KAN		
naka*ba*	kome	#	maki ma+		
r 24 s 5	r 119 s 6	r 18 s 8	r 49* s 9		

党	堂	常	掌	賞
political party	hall; temple	usual	control; palm (of hand)	prize
TŌ	DŌ	- JŌ	SHŌ	- SHŌ
#	#	tsune toko-	#	#
r 10* s 10	r 32 s 11	r 50 s 11	r 64 s 12	r 154 s 15

■□ 一

一

二	三	元	示	豆	言
two	three	origin	show	bean; miniature	say, speak; word
-	-				
NI	SAN	GEN GAN	SHI JI	TŌ ZU	GEN GON
futa*tsu* futa	mitsu mi'+ mi	moto	shime*su*	mame	i*u* koto
r 7　s 2	r 1　s 3	r 10　s 4	r 113　s 5	r 151　s 7	r 149　s 7

戸	戻	房	肩	雇	扉
door	return	room; tassel	shoulder	employ	door
-	-		-		
KO	REI	BŌ	KEN	KO	HI
to	modo*ru*..	fusa	kata	yato*u*	tobira
r 63　s 4	r 63　s 7	r 63　s 8	r 130　s 8	r 172　s 12	r 63　s 12

扇	遍	副	融		
fan (folding, electric)	widespread	secondary, deputy	melt, fuse; dissolve		
SEN	-				
ōgi	HEN	FUKU	YŪ		
r 63　s 10	#	#	#		
	r 162　s 12	r 18　s 11	r 142　s 16		

弐	武	頑	頭	顧	
two	military	stubborn	head; top	look back	
-	-	-	-		
NI	BU MU	GAN	TŌ ZU TO	KO	
#	#	#	atama kashira	kaeri*miru*	
r 56*　s 6	r 77　s 8	r 181　s 13	r 181　s 16	r 181　s 21	

丁	天	不	下		
city block; 4th; …	heaven, sky	not, un-	below, down		
CHŌ TEI	TEN	FU BU	KA GE		
#	ame ama-	#	shita moto shimo sa+ o+ kuda+		
r 1　s 2	r 37　s 4	r 1　s 4	r 1　s 3		

干	平	工	王	玉	正
dry	level; calm	industry; worker	king	jewel	correct
-			-	-	-
KAN	HEI BYŌ	KŌ KU	Ō	GYOKU	SHŌ SEI
hi*ru* ho+	hira tai+	#	#	tama	tada*su*.. masa
r 51　s 3	r 51　s 5	r 48　s 3	r 96　s 4	r 96　s 5	r 77　s 5

互	五	万	石	死	
mutual	five	ten thousand; many	stone	death	
-	-				
GO	GO	MAN BAN	SEKI SHAKU	SHI	
taga*i*	itsu itsu+	#	ishi	shi*nu*	
r 7　s 4	r 7　s 4	r 1*　s 3	r 112　s 5	r 78　s 6	

夏	憂	百	面		
summer	anxiety; sorrow	hundred	face, mask		
-					
KA GE	YŪ	HYAKU	MEN		
natsu	ure*eru*.. u+	#	omote omo tsura		
r 34*　s 10	r 61　s 15	r 106　s 6	r 176　s 9		

丙	両	雨	至	否	蚕
3rd	both	rain	arrive; utmost	negate	silkworm
-	-	-	SHI	-	-
HEI	RYŌ	U	ita*ru*	HI	SAN
#	#	ame ama-		ina	kaiko
r 1 s 5	r 1* s 6	r 173 s 8	r 133 s 6	r 30 s 7	r 142 s 10

更	再	画	璽		
renew; late	again; re-	picture; *kanji* stroke	imperial seal		
KŌ	SAI SA	GA KAKU	JI		
sara fu+	futata*bi*	#	#		
r 72* s 7	r 13 s 6	r 102 s 8	r 96 s 19		

雪	雲	霧	零	雷	電
snow	cloud	atmosphere	zero	thunder	electricity
-	-	-	-	-	-
SETSU	UN	FUN	REI	RAI	DEN
yuki	kumo	#	#	kaminari	#
r 173 s 11	r 173 s 12	r 173 s 12	r 173 s 13	r 173 s 13	r 173 s 13

需	霊	震	霜	露	霧
need, demand	spirit, soul	quake	frost	dew; exposed	fog
JU	REI RYŌ	-	-	RO RŌ	-
#	tama	SHIN	SŌ	tsuyu	MU
		furu*eru*..	shimo		kiri
r 173 s 14	r 173 s 15	r 173 s 15	r 173 s 17	r 173 s 21	r 173 s 19

西	亜	耳			
west	Asia; sub-	ear			
-	A	-			
SEI SAI	#	JI			
nishi		mimi			
r 146 s 6	r 7 s 7	r 128 s 6			

要	票	覆	覇		
essential	vote; chit	cover; topple	supremacy		
-	HYŌ	FUKU	-		
YŌ	#	ō*u* kutsugae+	HA		
i*ru*			#		
r 146 s 9	r 113 s 11	r 146 s 18	r 146 s 19		

亜	悪	遷			
Asia; sub-	bad, wicked	transition			
A	AKU O	-			
#	waru*i*	SEN			
r 7 s 7	r 61 s 11	#			
		r 162 s 15			

色 color — SHIKI SHOKU · iro · r 139 s 6

免 exemption — MEN · manuka*reru* · r 10 s 8

負 defeated; bear, suffer · FU · ma*keru*.. o+ · r 154 s 9

魚 fish — GYO · sakana uo · r 195 s 11

角 angle, corner · KAKU · kado tsuno · r 148 s 7

争 dispute — SŌ · araso*u* · r 6* s 6

危 dangerous — KI · abu*nai* aya+ · r 26 s 6

象 shape; elephant · SHŌ ZŌ · # · r 152 s 12

急 hurry; sudden · KYŪ · iso*gu* · r 61 s 9

逸 miss, let slip; deviate; excel · ITSU · # · r 162 s 11

冗 superfluous · JŌ · # · r 14 s 4

写 copy — SHA · utsu*su*.. · r 14* s 5

軍 army · GUN · # · r 159 s 9

冠 crown — KAN · kanmuri · r 14 s 9

欠 lack — KETSU · ka*ku*.. · r 76 s 4

運 transport; luck · UN · hako*bu* · r 162 s 12

気 spirit; air · KI KE · # · r 84 s 6

毎 every, each · MAI · # · r 80 s 6

午 noon — GO · # · r 24 s 4

年 year — NEN · toshi · r 51 s 6

缶 tin can — KAN · # · r 121 s 6

矢 arrow — SHI · ya · r 111 s 5

無 without, -less; not be · MU BU · na*i* · r 86 s 12

舞 dance — BU · ma*u* mai · r 136 s 15

欠 lack — KETSU · ka*ku*.. · r 76 s 4

行 go; do; line · GYŌ KŌ AN · *iku* yu+ okona+ · r 144 s 6

予 pre-, fore-; I · YO · # · r 6* s 4

矛 spear, lance · MU · hoko · r 110 s 5

柔 soft · JŪ NYŪ · yawa*raka*.. · r 75 s 9

勇 courage — YŪ · isa*mu* · r 19 s 9

通 pass; street; commute; ... · TSŪ TSU · tō*ru*.. kayo+ · r 162 s 10

了 finish; understand · RYŌ · # · r 6 s 2

子 child — SHI SU · ko · r 39 s 3

弁 speak, debate; valve; ... · BEN · # · r 55 s 5

台 pedestal; Taiwan · DAI TAI · # · r 30* s 5

怠 lazy; neglect · TAI · okota*ru* nama+ · r 61 s 9

参 visit; join in · SAN · mai*ru* · r 28 s 8

千	手	毛	乏	舌	系
thousand	hand	hair, fur	scarcity; poverty	tongue	lineage; group
-	-	-	BŌ	-	KEI
SEN	SHU	MŌ		ZETSU	#
chi	te ta	ke	toboshii	shita	
r 24 s 3	r 64 s 4	r 82 s 4	r 4 s 4	r 135 s 6	r 120 s 7

看	番	垂	乗	重
watch over	vigil; ranking	droop	ride	heavy; layered
-	-	-	-	JŪ CHŌ
KAN	BAN	SUI	JŌ	omoi kasa+ -e
#	#	tareru..	noru..	
r 109 s 9	r 102 s 12	r 32 s 8	r 4 s 9	r 166 s 9

妥	受	愛	爵
agree; calm	receive	love	peerage
DA	-	-	SHAKU
#	JU	AI	#
	ukeru..	#	
r 38 s 7	r 29 s 8	r 61 s 13	r 87 s 17

季	秀	委	香	番	透
season	excellent	entrust	fragrance	vigil; ranking	transparent
-	-	-	KŌ KYŌ	BAN	TŌ
KI	SHŪ	I	ka kao+	#	suku..
#	hiideru	#			
r 39 s 8	r 115 s 7	r 38 s 8	r 186 s 9	r 102 s 12	r 162 s 10

古 古 古 古 白

亡	立	文	交	六
deceased	stand, rise; set up	literature	intercourse	six
-	-	-	-	-
BŌ MŌ	RITSU RYŪ	BUN MON	KŌ	ROKU
na*i*	ta*tsu*..	fumi	ma*jiru* maji+ ka+	mu mu'+ mu+ mui
r 8 s 3	r 117 s 5	r 67 s 4	r 8 s 6	r 12 s 4

方	市	衣	玄	片
direction; side; person	city; market	garment	dark; occult	part, flake; single, one-
HŌ	SHI	-	GEN	HEN
kata	ichi	I	#	kata
r 70 s 4	r 50 s 5	koromo	r 95 s 5	r 91 s 4
		r 145 s 6		

夜	六
night	six
-	-
YA	ROKU
yoru yo	mu mu'+ mu+ mui
r 36 s 8	r 12 s 4

産
give birth
-
SAN
ubu u+
r 100 s 11

商	高
trade	high, tall; sum
-	KŌ
SHŌ	taka taka+
akina*u*	r 189 s 10
r 30 s 11	

卒	率	畜	衰	裏	褒
graduate; soldier	ratio; leader	livestock	decline	back, rear	praise
SOTSU	SOTSU RITSU	CHIKU	SUI	RI	HŌ
#	hiki*iru*	#	otoro*eru*	ura	ho*meru*
r 24 s 8	r 95 s 11	r 102 s 10	r 145 s 10	r 145 s 13	r 145 s 15

京	哀	享	亭	豪	高
capital city	pity, grief	enjoy; receive	inn	magnificent; Australia	high, tall; sum
KYŌ KEI	AI	KYŌ	-	GŌ	KŌ
#	awa*re*..	#	TEI	#	taka taka+
r 8 s 8	r 30 s 9	r 8 s 8	#	r 152 s 14	r 189 s 10
			r 8 s 9		

言
say, speak; word
GEN GON
i*u* koto
r 149 s 7

■ 宫 宫 宫 宫 宫 音

宫

京	哀	享	亭	豪	高
capital city	pity, grief	enjoy; receive	inn	magnificent; Australia	high, tall; sum
KYŌ KEI	AI	KYŌ	TEI	GŌ	KŌ
#	awa*re*..	#	#	#	taka taka+
r 8 s 8	r 30 s 9	r 8 s 8	r 8 s 9	r 152 s 14	r 189 s 10

宫

忘	妄	盲
forget	reckless	blind
-	-	-
BŌ	MŌ BŌ	MŌ
wasu*reru*	#	#
r 61 s 7	r 38 s 6	r 109 s 8

宫

充	育	棄
allot; fill	bring up (child)	abandon
JŪ	IKU	KI
a*teru*	soda*teru*..	#
r 10 s 6	r 130 s 8	r 75 s 13

宫

斉	斎
equal	purify; abstain from
-	-
SEI	SAI
#	#
r 67* s 8	r 67* s 11

宫

変	恋	蛮
alter; odd	romantic love	barbarian
HEN	REN	-
ka*waru*..	koi ko+ koi+	BAN
r 34* s 9	r 61 s 10	#
		r 142 s 12

音

辛	音	章	意	竜	童
spicy; hardship	sound	chapter; badge	intent; mind	dragon	child
SHIN	-	SHŌ	I	-	DŌ
kara*i*	ON IN	#	#	RYŪ	warabe
r 160 s 7	oto ne	r 117 s 11	r 61 s 13	tatsu	r 117 s 12
	r 180 s 9			r 117* s 10	

帝	産	商	適
emperor	give birth	trade	suitable
-	-	-	-
TEI	SAN	SHŌ	TEKI
#	ubu u+	akina*u*	#
r 50 s 9	r 100 s 11	r 30 s 11	r 162 s 14

穴	守	安	宅	宇	字
hole	protect	calm; cheap	home	cosmos	character, *kanji*, word
-	-	AN	-	-	JI
KETSU	SHU SU	yasu*i*	TAKU	U	aza
ana	mori mamo+	r 40 s 6	#	#	r 39 s 6
r 116 s 5	r 40 s 6		r 40 s 6	r 40 s 6	

家	実	宝	定
house; family	real, true; bear fruit	treasure	fix, decide
KA KE	JITSU	-	TEI JŌ
ie ya	mi mino+	HŌ	sada*meru..*
r 40 s 10	r 40 s 8	takara	r 40 s 8
		r 40 s 8	

宙	宜	官
sky, (outer) space	suitable; best wishes	official; government
CHŪ	GI	KAN
#	#	#
r 40 s 8	r 40 s 8	r 40 s 8

穴	宿	寝	寂	窃	窮
hole	inn, lodge	sleep	lonely	steal	extreme
-	-	-	-	-	-
KETSU	SHUKU	SHIN	JAKU SEKI	SETSU	KYŪ
ana	yado yado+	ne*ru..*	sabi sabi+	#	kiwa*maru..*
r 116 s 5	r 40 s 11	r 40 s 13	r 40 s 11	r 116 s 9	r 116 s 15

守
protect
-
SHU SU
mori mamo+
r 40 s 6

宀

宰 supervise, manage SAI # r 40 s 10	害 harm - GAI # r 40 s 10	憲 the law, constitution KEN # r 61 s 16	案 plan - AN # r 75 s 10	寄 approach; give KI yoru.. r 40 s 11	宵 dusk - SHŌ yoi r 40 s 10
寒 cold - KAN samui r 40 s 12	寛 tolerant - KAN # r 40 s 13	容 looks; contain YŌ # r 40 s 10	寧 calm - NEI # r 40 s 14	密 secret; dense; delicate MITSU # r 40 s 11	
審 trial - SHIN # r 40 s 15	客 guest, customer KYAKU KAKU # r 40 s 9	察 inspect; guess SATSU # r 40 s 14	寮 hostel, dormitory RYŌ # r 40 s 15		
官 official; government KAN # r 40 s 8	宮 shrine, palace KYŪ GŪ KU miya r 40 s 10	室 room - SHITSU muro r 40 s 9	宴 banquet - EN # r 40 s 10	賓 guest - HIN # r 154 s 15	寡 few; widow KA # r 40 s 14

宮

完 complete; perfect KAN # r 40 s 7	宗 religion - SHŪ SŌ # r 40 s 8	宣 announce - SEN # r 40 s 9	富 wealth - FU FŪ tomi to+ r 40 s 12
室 room - SHITSU muro r 40 s 9	賓 guest - HIN # r 154 s 15	寡 few; widow KA # r 40 s 14	

穴

空 air, sky; empty KŪ sora a+ kara r 116 s 8	究 research, investigate KYŪ kiwameru r 116 s 7	突 thrust - TOTSU tsuku r 116 s 8	容 looks; contain YŌ # r 40 s 10	
窓 window - SŌ mado r 116 s 11	窒 suffocate; plug - CHITSU # r 116 s 11	窯 kiln - YŌ kama r 116 s 15	窃 steal - SETSU # r 116 s 9	窮 extreme - KYŪ kiwamaru.. r 116 s 15

1	33
2	34
3	35
4	36
5	37
6	**38**
7	39
8	40
9	41
10	42
11	43
12	44
13	45
14	46
15	47
16	48
17	49
18	50
19	51
20	52
21	53
22	54
23	55
24	56
25	57
26	58
27	59
28	60
29	61
30	62
31	63
32	64

苎	芝	芋	英	苗	茂	芽
	turf	potato	talented; English	seedling	luxuriant, overgrown	bud
	-	-	EI	-	MO	GA
	#	#	#	BYŌ	shige*ru*	me
	shiba	imo		nae nawa		
	r 140 s 6	r 140 s 6	r 140 s 8	r 140 s 8	r 140 s 8	r 140 s 8
	芳	荒	苦	若	華	
	fragrant; (honorific) your	wild	pain; bitter	young	gorgeous; flowery; China	
	HŌ	KŌ	KU	JAKU NYAKU	KA KE	
	kanba*shii*	ara*i* a+	kuru*shii*.. niga+	waka*i* mo+	hana	
	r 140 s 7	r 140 s 9	r 140 s 8	r 140 s 8	r 140 s 10	

茁	花	荘	荷			
	flower	villa; sublime	load, cargo			
	-	SŌ	KA			
	KA	#	ni			
	hana					
	r 140 s 7	r 140 s 9	r 140 s 10			
	落	藩	藻	薄	薪	
	fall, drop	clan	seaweed	dilute, thin	firewood	
	RAKU	HAN	-	HAKU	SHIN	
	o*tosu*..	#	SŌ	usu*i*..	takigi	
			mo			
	r 140 s 12	r 140 s 18	r 140 s 19	r 140 s 16	r 140 s 16	

茁	若	薦	著			
	young	recommend	author; notable			
	-	SEN	CHO			
	JAKU NYAKU	susu*meru*	arawa*su* ichijiru+			
	waka*i* mo+					
	r 140 s 8	r 140 s 16	r 140 s 11			

茁	菊	茂				
	chrysan-themum	luxuriant, overgrown				
	KIKU	MO				
	#	shige*ru*				
	r 140 s 11	r 140 s 8				

茁	蔵	繭				
	store, keep	cocoon				
	ZŌ	-				
	kura	KEN				
		mayu				
	r 140 s 15	r 120 s 18				

茁	菌					
	germ; fungi					
	KIN					
	#					
	r 140 s 11					

▬ 苔

苦	芳	荒	蓄	著	
pain; bitter	fragrant; (honorific) your	wild	amass	author; notable	
KU	HŌ	KŌ	CHIKU	CHO	
kurushii.. niga+	kanbashii	arai a+	takuwaeru	arawasu ichijiru+	
r 140 s 8	r 140 s 7	r 140 s 9	r 140 s 13	r 140 s 11	

茶	菜	葉	薬	薫	
tea	vegetable	leaf	medicine, drug	fragrant	
CHA SA	SAI	YŌ	YAKU	KUN	
#	na	ha	kusuri	kaoru	
r 140 s 9	r 140 s 11	r 140 s 12	r 140 s 16	r 140 s 16	

芸	芽	茎	葬	蒸	華
art, skill	bud	stalk, stem	bury; funeral	steam; sultry	gorgeous; flowery; China
GEI	GA	KEI	SŌ	JŌ	KA KE
#	me	kuki	hōmuru	musu..	hana
r 140 s 7	r 140 s 8	r 140 s 8	r 140 s 12	r 140 s 13	r 140 s 10

草	墓	幕	慕	募	暮
grass, plants	grave, tomb	curtain; act (of play)	adore; yearn	raise funds, recruit	live; end; dusk
SŌ	BO	MAKU BAKU	BO	BO	BO
kusa	haka	#	shitau	tsunoru	kureru..
r 140 s 9	r 32 s 13	r 50 s 13	r 61 s 14	r 19 s 12	r 72 s 14

菓	夢				
candy, cake	dream				
KA	MU				
#	yume				
r 140 s 11	r 36 s 13				

共	昔	恭	黄	曹	遭
together; co-	ancient	respect	yellow	lawyer; companion	encounter
KYŌ	SEKI SHAKU	KYŌ	KŌ Ō	SŌ	SŌ
tomo	mukashi	uyauyashii	ki ko-	#	au
r 12 s 6	r 72 s 8	r 61 s 10	r 201 s 11	r 72* s 11	r 162 s 14

甘	井	某	革	鼓	賛
well (for water)	sweet	a certain (eg person)	leather; reform	drum	praise, approve
SEI SHŌ	KAN	BŌ	KAKU	KO	SAN
i	amai..	#	kawa	tsuzumi	#
r 7 s 4	r 99 s 5	r 75 s 9	r 177 s 9	r 207 s 13	r 154 s 15

土 十 圭 吉

土
soil, land;
Saturday
DO TO
tsuchi
r 32 s 3

士
warrior;
man
SHI
#
r 33 s 3

古
old,
antiquated
KO
furui..
r 30 s 5

克
overcome
-
KOKU
#
r 10 s 7

支
branch;
support
SHI
sasaeru
r 65 s 4

市
city;
market
SHI
ichi
r 50 s 5

直
directly;
fix
CHOKU JIKI
naosu.. tada+
r 109 s 8

真
true
-
SHIN
ma
r 109 s 10

索
cord;
seek
SAKU
#
r 120 s 10

南
south
-
NAN NA
minami
r 24 s 9

喪
mourning
-
SŌ
mo
r 30 s 12

衷
inmost
-
CHŪ
#
r 2* s 9

束
bundle
-
SOKU
taba
r 75 s 7

東
east
-
TŌ
higashi
r 75 s 8

車
vehicle
-
SHA
kuruma
r 159 s 7

恵
favor,
kindness
KEI E
megumu
r 61 s 10

専
exclusive
-
SEN
moppara
r 41 s 9

事
thing,
matter
JI ZU
koto
r 6 s 8

妻
wife
-
SAI
tsuma
r 38 s 8

去
depart;
past, gone
KYO KO
saru
r 28 s 5

寺
temple
-
JI
tera
r 41 s 6

走
run
-
SŌ
hashiru
r 156 s 7

赤
red
-
SEKI SHAKU
aka aka+
r 155 s 7

幸
happiness,
good fortune
KŌ
saiwai shiawa+ sachi
r 51 s 8

遠
distant
-
EN ON
tōi
r 162 s 13

達
achieve
-
TATSU
#
r 162 s 12

吉
lucky
-
KICHI KITSU
#
r 30 s 6

壱
one
-
ICHI
#
r 32* s 7

売
sell
-
BAI
uru..
r 32* s 7

声
voice
-
SEI SHŌ
koe kowa-
r 32* s 7

志
aspire,
intend
SHI
kokorozashi kokoroza+
r 61 s 7

喜
rejoice
-
KI
yorokobu
r 30 s 12

古
old
-
KO
furui..
r 30 s 5

克
overcome
-
KOKU
#
r 10 s 7

支
branch;
support
SHI
sasaeru
r 65 s 4

■□

毒	青	責	素	表	麦
poison	blue, green; young	blame; duty	basic, bare	surface; chart; display	cereal
-	SEI SHŌ	SEKI	SO SU	HYŌ	BAKU
DOKU	ao ao+	se*meru*	#	omote arawa+	mugi
#					
r 80　s 8	r 174　s 8	r 154　s 11	r 120　s 10	r 145　s 8	r 199　s 7

老	考	孝	者	煮
old age	consider	filial piety	person	boil, cook
-	-	KŌ	SHA	SHA
RŌ	KŌ	#	mono	ni*eru*..
o*iru* fu+	kanga*eru*			
r 125　s 6	r 125　s 6	r 39　s 7	r 125　s 8	r 86　s 12

占	点	卓	貞
divination; occupy	point, dot	eminent; desk	chastity
SEN	TEN	TAKU	-
urana*u* shi+	#	#	TEI
r 25　s 5	r 86*　s 9	r 24　s 8	#
			r 154　s 9

与	上
give	above, up
-	JŌ SHŌ
YO	ue kami uwa- a+ nobo+
ata*eru*	
r 1*　s 3	r 1　s 3

虐	虚	虞	虜	慮	膚
cruel	void	anxiety	captive	consider; concern for	skin
-	KYO KO	#	-	RYŌ	-
GYAKU	#	osore	RYO	#	FU
shiita*geru*			#		#
r 141　s 9	r 141　s 11	r 141　s 13	r 141　s 13	r 61　s 15	r 130　s 15

歩	肯	歯	歳
walk	agreement	tooth	year, years old
-	-	-	SAI SEI
HO BU FU	KŌ	SHI	#
aru*ku* ayu+	#	ha	
r 77　s 8	r 130　s 8	r 77*　s 12	r 77　s 13

共	昔	恭	黄
together; co-	ancient	respect	yellow
KYŌ	SEKI SHAKU	KYŌ	KŌ Ō
tomo	mukashi	uyauya*shii*	ki ko-
r 12　s 6	r 72　s 8	r 61　s 10	r 201　s 11

岩	炭	岸	崇	崩	出
rock, boulder	charcoal	shore	venerate	crumble	go out, exit; put out
GAN	-	GAN	SŪ	-	SHUTSU SUI
iwa	TAN	kishi	#	HŌ	de*ru* da+
r 46　s 8	sumi	r 46　s 8	r 46　s 11	kuzu*reru*..	
	r 86　s 8			r 46　s 11	r 17　s 5

1	33
2	34
3	35
4	36
5	37
6	38
7	39
8	**40**
9	41
10	42
11	43
12	44
13	45
14	46
15	47
16	48
17	49
18	50
19	51
20	52
21	53
22	54
23	55
24	56
25	57
26	58
27	59
28	60
29	61
30	62
31	63
32	64

夂 大 夫 关 木

夂	各 each - KAKU onoono r 30 s 6	冬 winter - TŌ fuyu r 15 s 5	条 clause - JŌ # r 75 s 7	多 many - TA ōi r 36 s 6	名 name; fame MEI MYŌ na r 30 s 6
大	奇 strange - KI # r 37 s 8	奔 hurry - HON # r 37 s 8	奪 snatch, rob DATSU ubau r 37 s 14	奮 inspired, excited FUN furuu r 37 s 16	太 thick; great TA TAI futoi.. r 37 s 4
夫	奉 offering; respectful HŌ BU tatematsuru r 37 s 8	奏 play music - SŌ kanaderu r 37 s 9	泰 tranquil - TAI # r 85 s 10	春 springtime - SHUN haru r 72 s 9	寿 longevity - JU kotobuki r 41* s 7
关	巻 roll; scroll; book KAN maki ma+ r 49* s 9	券 ticket - KEN # r 18 s 8			
木	査 investigate - SA # r 75 s 9	森 forest - SHIN mori r 75 s 12			

習	翌	翼
learn	next	wing
-	-	-
SHŪ	YOKU	YOKU
nara*u*	#	tsubasa
r 124　s 11	r 124　s 11	r 124　s 17

笛	笑	策	筆	第	篤
flute	laugh	plan, policy	writing brush	Number (as in 'Number 3')	good; seriously
-	-	-	-	-	-
TEKI	SHŌ	SAKU	HITSU	DAI	TOKU
fue	wara*u* e+	#	fude	#	#
r 118　s 11	r 118　s 10	r 118　s 12	r 118　s 12	r 118　s 11	r 118　s 16

答	管	等	算	築	符
answer	pipe; control	etc; equal; grade	calculate	construct, build	symbol; tag
-	-	-	-	-	-
TŌ	KAN	TŌ	SAN	CHIKU	FU
kota*e*..	kuda	hito*shii*	#	kizu*ku*	#
r 118　s 12	r 118　s 14	r 118　s 12	r 118　s 14	r 118　s 16	r 118　s 11

箱	節	範	筋	籍	簿
box	node, joint; season; …	model; norm; range	muscle, sinew	registration	record book
-	-	-	-	-	-
#	SETSU SECHI	HAN	KIN	SEKI	BO
hako	fushi	#	suji	#	#
r 118　s 15	r 118　s 13	r 118　s 15	r 118　s 12	r 118　s 20	r 118　s 19

簡	筒	箇	解	質	
simple, brief	tube	item	unravel; solve	quality; hostage	
-	-	-	-	-	
KAN	TŌ	KA	KAI GE	SHITSU SHICHI CHI	
#	tsutsu	#	to*ku*..	#	
r 118　s 18	r 118　s 12	r 118　s 14	r 148　s 13	r 154　s 15	

焦	集	隻	進
scorch; hasty	gather	one (of a pair)	advance
-	-	-	-
SHŌ	SHŪ	SEKI	SHIN
ko*gasu*.. ase+	tsudo*u* atsu+	#	susu*mu*..
r 86　s 12	r 172　s 12	r 172　s 10	r 162　s 11

雪	雲	雰	零	雷	電
snow	cloud	atmosphere	zero	thunder	electricity
-	-	-	-	-	-
SETSU	UN	FUN	REI	RAI	DEN
yuki	kumo	#	#	kaminari	#
r 173　s 11	r 173　s 12	r 173　s 12	r 173　s 13	r 173　s 13	r 173　s 13

需	霊	震	霜	露	霧
need, demand	spirit, soul	quake	frost	dew; exposed	fog
-	-	-	-	-	-
JU	REI RYŌ	SHIN	SŌ	RO RŌ	MU
#	tama	furu*eru*..	shimo	tsuyu	kiri
r 173　s 14	r 173　s 15	r 173　s 15	r 173　s 17	r 173　s 21	r 173　s 19

1	33
2	34
3	35
4	36
5	37
6	38
7	39
8	40
9	**41**
10	42
11	43
12	44
13	45
14	46
15	47
16	48
17	49
18	50
19	51
20	52
21	53
22	54
23	55
24	56
25	57
26	58
27	59
28	60
29	61
30	62
31	63
32	64

口

兄	号	呈	足
elder brother	number, designation	presentation	foot, leg; suffice
KEI KYŌ	GŌ	-	SOKU
ani	#	TEI	ashi ta+
r 10 s 5	r 30* s 5	#	r 157 s 7
		r 30 s 8	

品	呉	員
goods; grace	give; *Wu*	member
HIN	GO	-
shina	#	IN
r 30 s 9	r 30 s 7	r 30 s 10

日

早	昇	星	是	易	冒
early, swift	rise	star	right, just; this	easy; trade; divination	risk; defy
SŌ SA'	SHŌ	SEI SHŌ	ZE	EKI I	BŌ
haya*i*..	nobo*ru*	hoshi	#	yasa*shii*	okasu
r 72 s 6	r 72 s 8	r 72 s 9	r 72 s 9	r 72 s 8	r 109* s 9

昆	晶	最	暑	景	暴
insect	crystal	utmost	hot weather, summer	scenery	violent
-	-	-	SHO	-	-
KON	SHŌ	SAI	atsu*i*	KEI	BŌ BAKU
#	#	motto*mo*	r 72 s 12	#	aba*reru*..
r 72 s 8	r 72 s 12	r 72* s 12		r 72 s 12	r 72 s 15

量	曇	皇	泉
quantity	cloudy	emperor	spring; spa
-	-	-	SEN
RYŌ	DON	Ō KŌ	izumi
haka*ru*	kumo*ru*	#	r 85 s 9
r 166 s 12	r 72 s 16	r 106 s 9	

目

貝	具	見	県	且
shell; money	tool	see	prefecture	moreover, besides
#	-	-	-	#
kai	GU	KEN	KEN	ka*tsu*
r 154 s 7	#	mi*ru*..	#	r 1 s 5
	r 12 s 8	r 147 s 7	r 109* s 9	

身	息	臭
body; self	stinking	nose
SHIN	-	BI
mi	SHŪ	hana
r 158 s 7	kusa*i*	r 209 s 14
	r 132 s 9	

中

忠	患	貴	遺	遣
loyalty	ill	noble, valued	bequeath	send; spend; use
-	-	KI	-	KEN
CHŪ	KAN	tatto*i*.. tōto+	I YUI	tsuka*u*..
#	wazura*u*	r 154 s 12	#	r 162 s 13
r 61 s 8	r 61 s 11		r 162 s 15	

果	男	思	累	界	胃
fruit, result	male	think	accumulate	world; scope	stomach
-	-	-	-	-	-
KA	DAN NAN	SHI	RUI	KAI	I
ha*tasu*..	otoko	omo*u*	#	#	#
r 75　s 8	r 102　s 7	r 61　s 9	r 120　s 11	r 102　s 9	r 130　s 9

甲	里	畳	異	黒	愚
1st; shell	village; *ri*	fold up; *tatami* mat	different	black	foolish
KŌ KAN	RI	JŌ	I	KOKU	GU
#	sato	tatami tata+	koto koto+	kuro kuro+	oro*ka*
r 102　s 5	r 166　s 7	r 102　s 12	r 102　s 11	r 203　s 11	r 61　s 13

塁	墨	遇	卑	鬼	貫
fort; base (baseball)	India ink	meet; deal with	lowly	demon; ghost	pierce; carry through
RUI	BOKU	GŪ	HI	KI	KAN
#	sumi	#	iya*shii*..	oni	tsuranu*ku*
r 32　s 12	r 32　s 14	r 162　s 12	r 24　s 9	r 194　s 10	r 154　s 11

罪	買	置	署
crime	buy	put, place	signature; (police) station
-	-		
ZAI	BAI	CHI	SHO
tsumi	ka*u*	o*ku*	#
r 122　s 13	r 154　s 12	r 122　s 13	r 122　s 13

罰	羅	罷	還	衆	皿
punishment	net, gauze	stop work	return	the people	dish
-	-	-	-	-	-
BATSU BACHI	RA	HI	KAN	SHŪ SHU	#
#	#	#	#	#	sara
r 122　s 14	r 122　s 19	r 122　s 15	r 162　s 16	r 143　s 12	r 108　s 5

要	票	覆	覇
essential	vote; chit	cover; topple	supremacy
-	HYŌ	FUKU	-
YŌ	#	ō*u* kutsugae+	HA
i*ru*			#
r 146　s 9	r 113　s 11	r 146　s 18	r 146　s 19

亜	悪	遷
Asia; sub-	bad, wicked	transition
A	AKU O	-
#	waru*i*	SEN
r 7　s 7	r 61　s 11	#
		r 162　s 15

1	33
2	34
3	35
4	36
5	37
6	38
7	39
8	40
9	41
10	**42**
11	43
12	44
13	45
14	46
15	47
16	48
17	49
18	50
19	51
20	52
21	53
22	54
23	55
24	56
25	57
26	58
27	59
28	60
29	61
30	62
31	63
32	64

旨 gist	**帯** belt, sash; wear; zone	**貴** noble, valued	**遺** bequeath	**遣** send; spend; use
- SHI mune r 72 s 6	TAI obi o+ r 50 s 10	KI tatto*i*.. tōto+ r 154 s 12	- I YUI # r 162 s 15	KEN tsuka*u*.. r 162 s 13
粛 solemn; purge	**告** notify, announce	**先** ahead; previous	**脅** threaten	**炎** inflame
SHUKU # r 129 s 11	KOKU tsu*geru* r 30 s 7	SEN saki r 10 s 6	KYŌ obiya*kasu* odo+ r 130 s 10	EN honō r 86 s 8
皇 emperor	**泉** spring; spa	**息** breath; child	**臭** stinking	**鼻** nose
- ŌKŌ # r 106 s 9	SEN izumi r 85 s 9	SOKU iki r 61 s 10	- SHŪ kusa*i* r 132 s 9	- BI hana r 209 s 14
卑 lowly	**鬼** demon; ghost	**衆** the people		
- HI iya*shii*.. r 24 s 9	KI oni r 194 s 10	SHŪ SHU # r 143 s 12		
革 leather; reform	**某** a certain (eg person)	**基** foundations	**碁** *go* (the board game)	**甚** extremely
KAKU kawa r 177 s 9	BŌ # r 75 s 9	- KI moto motoi r 32 s 11	GO # r 112 s 13	- JIN hanaha*da*.. r 99 s 9
業 business; deed, act	**典** reference book	**豊** abundant	**農** farming	**曹** lawyer; companion
GYŌ GŌ waza r 75 s 13	TEN # r 12 s 8	- HŌ yuta*ka* r 151 s 13	- NŌ # r 161 s 13	SŌ # r 72* s 11
多 many	**名** name; fame	**無** without; -less; not be	**舞** dance	
- TA ō*i* r 36 s 6	MEI MYŌ na r 30 s 6	MU BU na*i* r 86 s 12	BU ma*u* mai r 136 s 15	
災 disaster	**希** rare; wish	**凶** misfortune; evil		
- SAI wazawa*i* r 86 s 7	KI # r 50 s 7	KYŌ # r 17 s 4		

Left-margin radical groupings:

ヒ 世 虫
丰 生 力 火
白 自
由 血
廿 甘 甚
业 曲 苗
夕 無
巛 乂

亡 不 天 云

貢	否	蚕	至
tribute	negate	silkworm	arrive; utmost
-	-	-	-
KŌ KU	HI	SAN	SHI
mitsu*gu*	ina	kaiko	ita*ru*
r 154 s 10	r 30 s 7	r 142 s 10	r 133 s 6

臣 百 凸 毋

悪	夏	憂	骨	貫
bad, wicked	summer	anxiety; sorrow	bone	pierce; carry through
AKU O	KA GE	YŪ	KOTSU	KAN
waru*i*	natsu	ure*eru*.. u+	hone	tsuranu*ku*
r 61 s 11	r 34* s 10	r 61 s 15	r 188 s 10	r 154 s 11

又 己 刀 刃

桑	忌	召	忍
mulberry	mourn; abhor	summon	endure; conceal
-	-	-	-
SŌ	KI	SHŌ	NIN
kuwa	i*mu*..	me*su*	shino*bu*..
r 75 s 10	r 61 s 7	r 30 s 5	r 61 s 7

ヨ 丰 尹 彑

尋	粛	君	長
inquire; normal	solemn; purge	lord; you	long; chief
JIN	SHUKU	KUN	CHŌ
tazu*neru*	#	kimi	naga*i*
r 41 s 12	r 129 s 11	r 30 s 7	r 168 s 8

正 幺 非

兵	岳	糸	悲	輩
soldier	mountain peak	thread	fellow, companion	sad
-	-	-	-	-
HEI HYŌ	GAKU	SHI	HAI	HI
#	take	ito	#	kana*shii*..
r 12 s 7	r 46 s 8	r 120 s 6	r 159 s 15	r 61 s 12

臼 匕マ 乂几

児	疑	殺
child	doubt	kill
-	-	-
JI NI	GI	SATSU SETSU SAI
#	utaga*u*	koro*su*
r 10 s 7	r 103 s 14	r 79 s 10

又 癶 所

祭	登	発	質
festival	climb	emit; start	quality; hostage
SAI	TŌ TO	HATSU HOTSU	SHITSU SHICHI CHI
matsu*ru*..	nobo*ru*	#	#
r 113 s 11	r 105 s 12	r 105 s 9	r 154 s 15

立 丽 吅吅 己

競	麗	器	選
compete	beautiful	container; utensil; skill	select
KYŌ KEI	REI	KI	SEN
kiso*u* se+	uruwa*shii*	utsuwa	era*bu*
r 117 s 20	r 198 s 19	r 30 s 15	r 162 s 15

1	33
2	34
3	35
4	36
5	37
6	38
7	39
8	40
9	41
10	42
11	**43**
12	44
13	45
14	46
15	47
16	48
17	49
18	50
19	51
20	52
21	53
22	54
23	55
24	56
25	57
26	58
27	59
28	60
29	61
30	62
31	63
32	64

一 ノ ハ ミ

ノ

少	歩	抄	秒	妙	砂
few	walk	excerpt	second (unit of time)	miraculous; odd	sand
-	-	-	-	-	-
SHŌ	HO BU FU	SHŌ	BYŌ	MYŌ	SA SHA
suko*shi* suku+	aru*ku* ayu+	#	#	#	suna
r 42 s 4	r 77 s 8	r 64 s 7	r 115 s 9	r 38 s 7	r 112 s 9

参
visit; join in
SAN
mai*ru*
r 28 s 8

、

太	勺	寸	冬	尽	寒
thick; great	*shaku*	tiny	winter	exhaust	cold
TA TAI	SHAKU	SUN	-	-	-
futo*i*..	#	#	TŌ	JIN	KAN
r 37 s 4	r 20 s 3	r 41 s 3	fuyu	tsu*kusu*..	samu*i*
			r 15 s 5	r 44* s 6	r 40 s 12

守	寿	等	寺	専	尊
protect	longevity	etc; equal; grade	temple	exclusive	esteem; your
-	-	-	-	-	-
SHU SU	JU	TŌ	JI	SEN	SON
mori mamo+	kotobuki	hito*shii*	tera	moppa*ra*	tatto*i*.. tōto+
r 40 s 6	r 41* s 7	r 118 s 12	r 41 s 6	r 41 s 9	r 41 s 12

奪	尋	導	辱
snatch, rob	inquire; normal	guide	disgrace, insult
DATSU	JIN	-	JOKU
uba*u*	tazu*neru*	DŌ	hazukashi*meru*
r 37 s 14	r 41 s 12	michibi*ku*	r 161 s 10
		r 41 s 15	

ミ

冬	尽	寒
winter	exhaust	cold
-	-	-
TŌ	JIN	KAN
fuyu	tsu*kusu*..	samu*i*
r 15 s 5	r 44* s 6	r 40 s 12

共 together; co- KYŌ tomo r 12 s 6	兵 soldier - HEI HYŌ # r 12 s 7

共 together; co-
KYŌ
tomo
r 12 s 6

兵 soldier
-
HEI HYŌ
#
r 12 s 7

呉 give; *Wu*
GO
#
r 30 s 7

穴 hole
-
KETSU
ana
r 116 s 5

六 six
-
ROKU
mu mu'+ mu+ mui
r 12 s 4

貝 shell; money
#
kai
r 154 s 7

具 tool
-
GU
#
r 12 s 8

典 reference book
TEN
#
r 12 s 8

真 true
-
SHIN
ma
r 109 s 10

黄 yellow
-
KŌ Ō
ki ko-
r 201 s 11

異 different
-
I
koto koto+
r 102 s 11

翼 wing
-
YOKU
tsubasa
r 124 s 17

興 prosper; fun
KYŌ KŌ
okoru..
r 134 s 16

貞 chastity
-
TEI
#
r 154 s 9

負 defeated; bear, suffer
FU
ma*keru*.. o+
r 154 s 9

貢 tribute
-
KŌ KU
mitsu*gu*
r 154 s 10

員 member
-
IN
#
r 30 s 10

買 buy
-
BAI
ka*u*
r 154 s 12

貴 noble, valued
KI
tatto*i*.. tōto+
r 154 s 12

貫 pierce; carry through
KAN
tsuranu*ku*
r 154 s 11

責 blame; duty
SEKI
se*meru*
r 154 s 11

費 cost
-
HI
tsui*yasu*..
r 154 s 12

賞 prize
-
SHŌ
#
r 154 s 15

賓 guest
-
HIN
#
r 154 s 15

貧 poverty
-
HIN BIN
mazu*shii*
r 154 s 11

貨 goods; coin, money
KA
#
r 154 s 11

貸 lend, rent out
TAI
ka*su*
r 154 s 12

賃 fee, wages
CHIN
#
r 154 s 13

資 assets
-
SHI
#
r 154 s 13

賛 praise, approve
SAN
#
r 154 s 15

賀 good wishes
-
GA
#
r 154 s 12

貿 trade
-
BŌ
#
r 154 s 12

賢 wise
-
KEN
kashiko*i*
r 154 s 16

質 quality; hostage
SHITSU SHICHI CHI
#
r 154 s 15

欠 lack
-
KETSU
ka*ku*..
r 76 s 4

久 long time
-
KYŪ KU
hisa*shii*
r 4 s 3

英 talented; English
EI
#
r 140 s 8

肉 meat, flesh
-
NIKU
#
r 130 s 6

腐 rot
-
FU
kusa*ru*..
r 130 s 14

虞 anxiety
-
#
osore
r 141 s 13

1	33
2	34
3	35
4	36
5	37
6	38
7	39
8	40
9	41
10	42
11	43
12	**44**
13	45
14	46
15	47
16	48
17	49
18	50
19	51
20	52
21	53
22	54
23	55
24	56
25	57
26	58
27	59
28	60
29	61
30	62
31	63
32	64

儿

元	光	先	児	兄	見
origin	light	ahead; previous	child	elder brother	see
-	-	-	-	-	-
GEN GAN	KŌ	SEN	JI NI	KEI KYŌ	KEN
moto	hikari hika+	saki	#	ani	mi*ru*..
r 10 s 4	r 10 s 6	r 10 s 6	r 10 s 7	r 10 s 5	r 147 s 7

克	充	完	売	党	免
overcome	allot; fill	complete; perfect	sell	political party	exemption
KOKU	JŪ	KAN	BAI	TŌ	MEN
#	a*teru*	#	u*ru*..	#	manuka*reru*
r 10 s 7	r 10 s 6	r 40 s 7	r 32* s 7	r 10* s 10	r 10 s 8

覚	寛	覧	穴	冗	英
memorize; awake	tolerant	look at	hole	superfluous	talented; English
KAKU	KAN	RAN	KETSU	JŌ	EI
obo*eru* sa+	#	#	ana	#	#
r 147 s 12	r 40 s 13	r 147 s 17	r 116 s 5	r 14 s 4	r 140 s 8

冠	鬼	荒	発	廃	魔
crown	demon; ghost	wild	emit; start	obsolete, waste, scrap	demon, devil
-	KI	-	HATSU HOTSU	HAI	MA
KAN	oni	KŌ	#	suta*reru*..	#
kanmuri		arai a+			
r 14 s 9	r 194 s 10	r 140 s 9	r 105 s 9	r 53 s 12	r 194 s 21

儿

介	界	斉	斎	粛
mediate	world; scope	equal	purify; abstain from	solemn; purge
KAI	KAI	SEI	SAI	SHUKU
#	#	#	#	#
r 9 s 4	r 102 s 9	r 67* s 8	r 67* s 11	r 129 s 11

艹

弁	升	昇	奔	算	鼻
speak, debate; valve; ...	*sho*; measure	rise	hurry	calculate	nose
BEN	SHŌ	SHŌ	HON	SAN	BI
#	masu	nobo*ru*	#	#	hana
r 55 s 5	r 24 s 4	r 72 s 8	r 37 s 8	r 118 s 14	r 209 s 14

葬	弊	戒	開	発	廃
bury; funeral	evil; our/my humble	warn; command	open	emit; start	obsolete, waste, scrap
SŌ	HEI	KAI	KAI	HATSU HOTSU	HAI
hōmu*ru*	#	imashi*meru*	a*keru*.. hira+	#	suta*reru*..
r 140 s 12	r 55 s 15	r 62 s 7	r 169 s 12	r 105 s 9	r 53 s 12

匕

壱	老	尼
one	old age	nun
-	-	-
ICHI	RŌ	NI
#	oi*ru* fu+	ama
r 32* s 7	r 125 s 6	r 44 s 5

寸

守 protect - SHU SU mori mamo+ r 40　s 6	寿 longevity - JU kotobuki r 41*　s 7	等 etc; equal; grade TŌ hito*shii* r 118　s 12	寺 temple - JI tera r 41　s 6	専 exclusive - SEN moppa*ra* r 41　s 9	尊 esteem; your SON tatto*i*.. tōto+ r 41　s 12
奪 snatch, rob DATSU uba*u* r 37　s 14	尋 inquire; normal JIN tazu*neru* r 41　s 12	導 guide - DŌ michibi*ku* r 41　s 15	辱 disgrace, insult JOKU hazukashi*meru* r 161　s 10		

十

千 thousand - SEN chi r 24　s 3	午 noon - GO # r 24　s 4	干 dry - KAN hi*ru* ho+ r 51　s 3	革 leather; reform KAKU kawa r 177　s 9	卑 lowly - HI iya*shii*.. r 24　s 9	
卒 graduate; soldier SOTSU # r 24　s 8	率 ratio; leader SOTSU RITSU hiki*iru* r 95　s 11	辛 spicy; hardship SHIN kara*i* r 160　s 7	宰 supervise, manage SAI # r 40　s 10	幸 happiness, good fortune KŌ saiwa*i* shiawa+ sachi r 51　s 8	
早 early, swift SŌ SA' haya*i*.. r 72　s 6	卓 eminent; desk TAKU # r 24　s 8	草 grass, plants SŌ kusa r 140　s 9	単 single, simple TAN # r 24*　s 9	章 chapter; badge SHŌ # r 117　s 11	
傘 umbrella - SAN kasa r 9　s 12	華 gorgeous; flowery; China KA KE hana r 140　s 10	準 norm; quasi- JUN # r 85　s 13	軍 army - GUN # r 159　s 9	輩 fellow, companion HAI # r 159　s 15	

巾

市 city; market SHI ichi r 50　s 5	帝 emperor - TEI # r 50　s 9	帯 belt, sash; wear; zone TAI obi o+ r 50　s 10	常 usual - JŌ tsune toko- r 50　s 11	幕 curtain; act (of play) MAKU BAKU # r 50　s 13	幣 money - HEI # r 50　s 15
布 cloth; spread FU nuno r 50　s 5	希 rare; wish KI # r 50　s 7	席 seat, place SEKI # r 50　s 10			

小

京	景	寮	県	糸	系
capital city	scenery	hostel, dormitory	prefecture	thread	lineage; group
KYŌ KEI	- KEI	- RYŌ	- KEN	- SHI ito	- KEI
#	#	#	#		#
r8 s8	r72 s12	r40 s15	r109* s9	r120 s6	r120 s7

乗	余	茶	荒
ride	remainder; surplus	tea	wild
- JŌ noru..	- YO amaru..	- CHA SA	- KŌ arai a+
r4 s9	r9 s7	# r140 s9	# r140 s9

原	療	斎
prairie; origin	treat illness	purify; abstain from
GEN hara	- RYŌ	SAI
r27 s10	# r104 s17	# r67* s11

示

示	宗	票	崇
show	religion	vote; chit	venerate
- SHI JI shimesu	- SHŪ SŌ	- HYŌ	- SŪ
r113 s5	# r40 s8	# r113 s11	# r46 s11

禁	祭	察
prohibit	festival	inspect; guess
KIN	- SAI matsuru..	SATSU
# r113 s13	r113 s11	# r40 s14

水

泉	暴	泰	康	尿	衆
spring; spa	violent	tranquil	healthy; safe	urine	the people
SEN izumi	- BŌ BAKU abareru..	- TAI	- KŌ	- NYŌ	- SHŪ SHU
r85 s9	r72 s15	# r85 s10	# r53 s11	# r44 s7	# r143 s12

糸

系	素	索	累
lineage; group	basic, bare	cord; seek	accumulate
KEI	- SO SU	- SAKU	- RUI
# r120 s7	# r120 s10	# r120 s10	# r120 s11

紫	緊	繁
purple	tight	flourishing
- SHI murasaki	- KIN	- HAN
r120 s12	# r120 s15	# r120 s16

分	券	雰	寡	秀	
portion; minutes	ticket	atmosphere	few; widow	excellent	
BU FUN BUN	KEN	FUN	KA	SHŪ	
wa*keru*..	#	#	#	hii*deru*	
r 18　s 4	r 18　s 8	r 173　s 12	r 40　s 14	r 115　s 7	
労	劣	男	勇	募	努
labor	inferior	male	courage	raise funds, recruit	effort
RŌ	RETSU	DAN NAN	YŪ	BO	DO
#	oto*ru*	otoko	isa*mu*	tsuno*ru*	tsuto*meru*
r 19　s 7	r 19　s 6	r 102　s 7	r 19　s 9	r 19　s 12	r 19　s 7
勢	虜	万	方	芳	房
power; tendency	captive	ten thousand; many	direction; side; person	fragrant; (honorific) your	room; tassel
SEI	RYO	MAN BAN	HŌ	HŌ	BŌ
Ikio*i*	#	#	kata	kanba*shii*	fusa
r 19　s 13	r 141　s 13	r 1*　s 3	r 70　s 4	r 140　s 7	r 63　s 8
果	某	栄	菜	菓	巣
fruit, result	a certain (eg person)	glory; prosper	vegetable	candy, cake	nest
KA	BŌ	EI	SAI	KA	SŌ
ha*tasu*..	#	hae.. saka+	na	#	su
r 75　s 8	r 75　s 9	r 75　s 9	r 140　s 11	r 140　s 11	r 75*　s 11
条	柔	案	棄	集	業
clause	soft	plan	abandon	gather	business; deed, act
JŌ	JŪ NYŪ	AN	KI	SHŪ	GYŌ GŌ
#	yawa*raka*..	#	#	tsudo*u* atsu+	waza
r 75　s 7	r 75　s 10	r 75　s 10	r 75　s 13	r 172　s 12	r 75　s 13
葉	薬	染	架		
leaf	medicine, drug	dye	beam, frame; span (gap)		
YŌ	YAKU	SEN	KA		
ha	kusuri	so*meru*.. shi+	ka*keru*..		
r 140　s 12	r 140　s 16	r 75　s 9	r 75　s 9		
楽	桑	築			
music; joy	mulberry	construct, build			
GAKU RAKU	SŌ	CHIKU			
tano*shii*..	kuwa	kizu*ku*			
r 75　s 13	r 75　s 10	r 118　s 16			
床	閑	米	茶		
bed; floor	leisure	rice; America	tea		
SHŌ	KAN	BEI MAI	CHA SA		
toko yuka	#	kome	#		
r 53　s 7	r 169　s 12	r 119　s 6	r 140　s 9		

1	33
2	34
3	35
4	36
5	37
6	38
7	39
8	40
9	41
10	42
11	43
12	44
13	45
14	**46**
15	47
16	48
17	49
18	50
19	51
20	52
21	53
22	54
23	55
24	56
25	57
26	58
27	59
28	60
29	61
30	62
31	63
32	64

立 业 灬 小

立

立 stand, rise, set up
RITSŪ RYU
ta*tsu*..
r 117 s 5

豆 bean; miniature
TŌ ZU
mame
r 151 s 7

翌 next
-
YOKU
#
r 124 s 11

登 climb
-
TŌ TO
nobo*ru*
r 105 s 12

豊 abundant
-
HŌ
yuta*ka*
r 151 s 13

痘 smallpox
-
TŌ
#
r 104 s 12

业

並 line up; ordinary
HEI
nara*bu*.. nami
r 1* s 8

霊 spirit, soul
-
REI RYŌ
tama
r 173 s 15

虚 void
-
KYO KO
#
r 141 s 11

灬

点 point, dot
TEN
#
r 86* s 9

魚 fish
-
GYO
sakana uo
r 195 s 11

無 without, -less; not be
MU BU
na*i*
r 86 s 12

焦 scorch; hasty
SHŌ
ko*gasu*.. ase+
r 86 s 12

馬 horse
-
BA
uma ma
r 187 s 10

鳥 bird
-
CHŌ
tori
r 196 s 11

黒 black
-
KOKU
kuro kuro+
r 203 s 11

煮 boil, cook
-
SHA
ni*eru*..
r 86 s 12

薫 fragrant
-
KUN
kao*ru*
r 140 s 16

蒸 steam; sultry
JŌ
mu*su*..
r 140 s 13

窯 kiln
-
YŌ
kama
r 116 s 15

為 do; purpose I
#
r 86* s 9

烈 intense
-
RETSU
#
r 86 s 10

照 shine; embarrassed
SHŌ
te*ru*..
r 86 s 13

然 -like; nature
ZEN NEN
#
r 86 s 12

黙 silent
-
MOKU
dama*ru*
r 203 s 15

勲 meritorious
-
KUN
#
r 19 s 15

熱 heat; fever
-
NETSU
atsu*i*
r 86 s 15

熟 mature
-
JUKU
u*reru*
r 86 s 15

庶 multitude
-
SHO
#
r 53 s 11

薦 recommend
-
SEN
susu*meru*
r 140 s 16

小

恭 respect
-
KYŌ
uyauya*shii*
r 61 s 10

慕 adore; yearn
BO
shita*u*
r 61 s 14

 心

忌	忠	患	忍	志	
mourn; abhor	loyalty	ill	endure; conceal	aspire, intend	
KI	- CHŪ	- KAN	NIN	SHI	
i*mu..*	#	wazura*u*	shino*bu..*	kokorozashi kokoroza+	
r 61 s 7	r 61 s 8	r 61 s 11	r 61 s 7	r 61 s 7	

忘	恋	思	恩	悪	恵
forget	romantic love	think	grace; favor	bad, wicked	favor, kindness
- BŌ	REN	- SHI	ON	AKU O	KEI E
wasu*reru*	koi ko+ koi+	omo*u*	#	waru*i*	megu*mu*
r 61 s 7	r 61 s 10	r 61 s 9	r 61 s 10	r 61 s 11	r 61 s 10

忘	恋	急	念	息	怠
forget	romantic love	hurry; sudden	thought; desire	breath; child	lazy; neglect
- BŌ	REN	KYŪ	NEN	SOKU	TAI
wasu*reru*	koi ko+ koi+	iso*gu*	#	iki	okota*ru* nama+
r 61 s 7	r 61 s 10	r 61 s 9	r 61 s 9	r 61 s 10	r 61 s 9

愚	意	窓	憲	慈	
foolish	intent; mind	window	the law, constitution	compassion	
- GU	I	- SŌ	KEN	- JI	
oro*ka*	#	mado	#	itsuku*shimu*	
r 61 s 13	r 61 s 13	r 116 s 11	r 61 s 16	r 61 s 13	

悲	恐	怒	想	愁	悠
sad	fear	anger	thought	sorrow	relax
- HI	- KYŌ	- DO	- SŌ SO	SHŪ	- KEI
kana*shii..*	oso*reru..*	oko*ru* ika+	#	ure*i..*	iko*i..*
r 61 s 12	r 61 s 10	r 61 s 9	r 61 s 13	r 61 s 13	r 61 s 16

憩	懸	慰	懇	態	懲
relaxed; far	hang; risk	console, cheer up	intimate; kind; polite; sincere	appearance; state, condition	punish, chastise
YŪ	KEN KE	I	KON	TAI	CHŌ
#	ka*karu..*	nagusa*meru*	nengo*ro*	#	ko*rasu..*
r 61 s 11	r 61 s 20	r 61 s 15	r 61 s 17	r 61 s 14	r 61 s 18

惑	感	恩	思
astray; mislead	senses; feel	grace; favor	think
WAKU	KAN	ON	- SHI
mado*u*	#	#	omo*u*
r 61 s 12	r 61 s 13	r 61 s 10	r 61 s 9

応	慮	癒
respond	consider; concern for	heal
- Ō	- RYO	- YU
#	#	#
r 61 s 7	r 61 s 15	r 104 s 18

一

| 二 two - NI futatsu futa r7 s2 | 三 three - SAN mitsu mi'+ mi r1 s3 | 立 stand, rise, set up RITSU RYU tatsu.. r117 s5 | 豆 bean; miniature TŌ ZU mame r151 s7 | 登 climb - TŌ TO noboru r105 s12 | 豊 abundant - HŌ yutaka r151 s13 |

| 翌 next - YOKU # r124 s11 | 昼 daytime, noon CHŪ hiru r72 s9 | 宣 announce - SEN # r40 s9 | 宜 suitable; best wishes GI # r40 s8 | 査 investigate - SA # r75 s9 | 畳 fold up; tatami mat JŌ tatami tata+ r102 s12 |

| 弐 two - NI # r56* s6 | 邸 mansion - TEI # r163 s8 | 底 bottom, base TEI soko r53 s8 | 痘 smallpox - TŌ # r104 s12 | 極 extremes - KYOKU GOKU kiwami.. r75 s12 |

| 土 soil, land; Saturday DO TO tsuchi r32 s3 | 士 warrior; man SHI # r33 s3 | 止 stop - SHI tomaru.. r77 s4 | 上 above, up JŌ SHŌ ue kami uwa- a+ nobo+ r1 s3 |

| 工 industry; worker KŌ KU # r48 s3 | 王 king - Ō # r96 s4 | 玉 jewel - GYOKU tama r96 s5 | 正 correct - SHŌ SEI tadasu.. masa r77 s5 | 生 life; birth; grow; raw SHŌ SEI nama i+ u+ ha+ o+ ki- r100 s5 |

| 五 five - GO itsu itsu+ r7 s4 | 互 mutual - GO tagai r7 s4 | 丘 hill - KYŪ oka r1 s5 | 並 line up; ordinary HEI narabu.. nami r1* s8 | 霊 spirit, soul REI RYŌ tama r173 s15 | 虚 void - KYO KO # r141 s11 |

| 且 moreover, besides # katsu r1 s5 | 皿 dish - # sara r108 s5 | 血 blood - KETSU chi r143 s6 | 益 benefit - EKI YAKU # r108 s10 | 盆 tray - BON # r108 s9 | 盛 prosperous; heap up SEI JŌ sakaru.. mo+ r108 s11 |

| 盗 steal - TŌ nusumu r108 s11 | 盟 alliance - MEI # r108 s13 | 監 oversee - KAN # r108 s15 | 盤 disk; tray, board, base BAN # r108 s15 |

山　土　止

出	缶	岳	両	密
go out, exit; put out	tin can	mountain peak	both	secret; dense; delicate
SHUTSU SUI	-	GAKU	-	MITSU
de*ru* da+	KAN	take	RYŌ	#
r 17　s 5	r 121　s 6	r 46　s 8	r 1*　s 6	r 40　s 11

屈	島	幽		
bend; yield	island	deep; hidden; remote; …		
KUTSU	-	YŪ		
#	TŌ	#		
r 44　s 8	shima	r 52　s 9		
	r 46　s 10			

里	堂	至	室	窒	重
village;	hall; temple	arrive; utmost	room	suffocate; plug	heavy; layered
ri	DŌ	SHI	-	CHITSU	JŪ CHŌ
RI	#	ita*ru*	SHITSU	#	omo*i* kasa+ -e
sato	r 32　s 11	r 133　s 6	muro	r 116　s 11	r 166　s 9
r 166　s 7			r 40　s 9		

茎	墓	基	塁	墨
stalk, stem	grave, tomb	foundations	fort; base (baseball)	India ink
KEI	BO	-	RUI	BOKU
kuki	haka	KI	#	sumi
r 140　s 8	r 32　s 13	moto motoi	r 32　s 12	r 32　s 14
		r 32　s 11		

型	堅	塗	墜	堕
template	firm, hard	paint	fall, drop	degenerate
-	KEN	TO	TSUI	DA
KEI	kata*i*	nu*ru*	#	#
kata	r 32　s 12	r 32　s 13	r 32　s 15	r 32　s 12
r 32　s 9				

塑	墾	壁	塾	圧	在
model, molding	clear land, cultivate	wall	cram school	pressure	be located; exist; suburbs
SO	KON	-	JUKU	-	ZAI
#	#	HEKI	#	ATSU	a*ru*
r 32　s 13	r 32　s 16	kabe	r 32　s 14	#	r 32　s 6
		r 32　s 16		r 32　s 5	

座	屋	厘	童	量
sit, seat	house; -seller	*rin*	child	quantity
ZA	OKU	-	-	-
suwa*ru*	ya	RIN	DŌ	RYŌ
r 53　s 10	r 44　s 9	#	warabe	haka*ru*
		r 27　s 9	r 117　s 12	r 166　s 12

企	整	武	歴	症
plan	arrange	military	history, career, CV.	symptoms
-	SEI	BU MU	REKI	SHŌ
KI	totono*eru*..	#	#	#
kuwada*teru*	r 66　s 16	r 77　s 8	r 77　s 14	r 104　s 10
r 9　s 6				

1	33
2	34
3	35
4	36
5	37
6	38
7	39
8	40
9	41
10	42
11	43
12	44
13	45
14	46
15	47
16	**48**
17	49
18	50
19	51
20	52
21	53
22	54
23	55
24	56
25	57
26	58
27	59
28	60
29	61
30	62
31	63
32	64

乂 又 夂 女

文	父	交
literature	father	intercourse
-	-	-
BUN MON	FU	KŌ
fumi	chichi	majiru maji+ ka+
r 67 s 4	r 88 s 4	r 8 s 6

気	茂	及	勺
spirit; air	luxuriant, overgrown	attain	monme
KI KE	MO	KYŪ	-
#	shigeru	oyobu..	#
r 84 s 6	r 140 s 8	r 29 s 3	monme
			r 20 s 4

又

支	受	隻	反	友	皮
branch; support	receive	one (of a pair)	oppose; bend, warp	friend	skin
SHI	JU	SEKI	HAN HON TAN	YŪ	HI
sasaeru	ukeru..	#	soru..	tomo	kawa
r 65 s 4	r 29 s 8	r 172 s 10	r 29 s 4	r 29 s 4	r 107 s 5

度	疫	疲	髪
degree, extent; times; ...	epidemic	fatigue	hair
DO TAKU TO	EKI YAKU	HI	HATSU
tabi	#	tsukareru..	kami
r 53 s 9	r 104 s 9	r 104 s 10	r 190 s 14

夂

麦	変	夏	憂	愛	慶
cereal	alter; odd	summer	anxiety; sorrow	love	celebrate
BAKU	HEN	KA GE	YŪ	AI	KEI
mugi	kawaru..	natsu	ureeru.. u+	#	#
r 199 s 7	r 34* s 9	r 34* s 10	r 61 s 15	r 61 s 13	r 61 s 15

女

安	妄	妥	委	要
calm; cheap	reckless	agree; calm	entrust	essential
AN	MŌ BŌ	DA	I	YŌ
yasui	#	#	#	iru
r 40 s 6	r 38 s 6	r 38 s 7	r 38 s 8	r 146 s 9

宴	妻	姿	婆
banquet	wife	figure	old woman
-	-	-	-
EN	SAI	SHI	BA
#	tsuma	sugata	#
r 40 s 10	r 38 s 8	r 38 s 9	r 38 s 11

走 run - SŌ hashi*ru* r 156 s 7	**足** foot, leg; suffice SOKU ashi ta+ r 157 s 7	**是** right, just; this ZE # r 72 s 9	**定** fix, decide TEI JŌ sada*meru*.. r 40 s 8		
災 disaster - SAI wazawa*i* r 86 s 7	**炎** inflame - EN honō r 86 s 8	**灰** ash - KAI hai r 86 s 6	**炭** charcoal - TAN sumi r 86 s 9		
突 thrust - TOTSU tsu*ku* r 116 s 8	**臭** stinking - SHŪ kusa*i* r 132 s 9	**奥** inmost, core - Ō oku r 37 s 12	**奨** encourage - SHŌ # r 37 s 13	**契** pledge - KEI chigi*ru* r 37 s 9	**喫** eat, drink, smoke KITSU r 30 s 12
天 heaven, sky TEN ame ama- r 37 s 4	**矢** arrow - SHI ya r 111 s 5	**笑** laugh - SHŌ wara*u* e+ r 118 s 10	**奏** play music - SŌ kana*deru* r 37 s 9	**美** beauty - BI utsuku*shii* r 123 s 9	**戻** return - REI modo*ru*.. r 63 s 7
空 air, sky; empty KŪ sora a+ kara r 116 s 8	**式** rite; style SHIKI # r 56 s 6	**左** left (hand) SA hidari r 48 s 5	**差** difference - SA sa*su* r 48 s 10		
主 master - SHU SU nushi omo r 3 s 5	**全** whole - ZEN matta*ku* r 9* s 6	**呈** presentation - TEI # r 30 s 8	**皇** emperor - Ō KŌ # r 106 s 9	**望** hope; view BŌ MŌ nozo*mu* r 130* s 11	**聖** holy - SEI # r 128 s 13
星 star - SEI SHŌ hoshi r 72 s 9	**産** give birth - SAN ubu u+ r 100 s 11	**宝** treasure - HŌ takara r 40 s 8	**璽** imperial seal JI # r 96 s 19		

1	33
2	34
3	35
4	36
5	37
6	38
7	39
8	40
9	41
10	42
11	43
12	44
13	45
14	46
15	47
16	48
17	**49**
18	50
19	51
20	52
21	53
22	54
23	55
24	56
25	57
26	58
27	59
28	60
29	61
30	62
31	63
32	64

□ 丁 于 子 手

丁

予 pre-, fore-; | YO # r 6* s 4

亭 inn - TEI # r 8 s 9

寧 calm - NEI # r 40 s 14

庁 government agency CHŌ # r 53 s 5

序 preface; rank, order JO # r 53 s 7

斤 *kin* - KIN # r 69 s 4

子 child - SHI SU ko r 39 s 3

于

宇 cosmos - U # r 40 s 6

芋 potato - # imo r 140 s 6

辛 spicy; hardship SHIN kara*i* r 160 s 7

宰 supervise, manage SAI # r 40 s 10

幸 happiness, good fortune KŌ saiwa*i* shiawa+ sachi r 51 s 8

岸 shore - GAN kishi r 46 s 8

南 south - NAN NA minami r 24 s 9

子

字 character, *kanji*, word JI aza r 39 s 6

学 study, learning GAKU mana*bu* r 39 s 8

享 enjoy; receive KYŌ # r 8 s 8

季 season - KI # r 39 s 8

孝 filial piety KŌ # r 39 s 7

存 exist; think that SON ZON # r 39 s 6

厚 thick; cordial KŌ atsu*i* r 27 s 9

手

挙 raise; arrest; whole; ... KYO a*geru*.. r 64 s 10

掌 control; palm (of hand) SHŌ # r 64 s 12

撃 strike, attack GEKI u*tsu* r 64 s 15

摩 rub - MA # r 64 s 15

公	玄	去	広		
public; official	dark; occult	depart; past, gone	wide		
-	-	-	-		
KŌ	GEN	KYO KO	KŌ		
ōyake	#	saru	hiroi..		
r 12 s 4	r 95 s 5	r 28 s 5	r 53 s 5		
会	芸	雲	曇		
meet	art, skill	cloud	cloudy		
-	-	-	-		
KAI E	GEI	UN	DON		
au	#	kumo	kumoru		
r 9* s 6	r 140 s 7	r 173 s 12	r 72 s 16		
衣	衰	衷	哀		
garment	decline	inmost	pity, grief		
-	-	-	-		
I	SUI	CHŪ	AI		
koromo	otoroeru	#	aware..		
r 145 s 6	r 145 s 10	r 2* s 9	r 30 s 9		
表	裏	褒			
surface; chart; display	back, rear	praise			
HYŌ	RI	-			
omote arawa+	ura	HŌ			
r 145 s 8	r 145 s 13	homeru			
		r 145 s 15			
袋	装	裂	製	襲	裁
bag	put on, wear; equip	split	manufacture	raid; inherit	judge; cut
-	SŌ SHŌ	-	-	SHŪ	SAI
TAI	yosōu	RETSU	SEI	osou	sabaku ta+
fukuro	r 145 s 12	sakeru..	#	r 145 s 22	r 145 s 12
r 145 s 11		r 145 s 12	r 145 s 14		
長	喪	展	農	震	養
long; chief	mourning	display, unfold	farming	quake	foster, rear
CHŌ	-	TEN	-	-	YŌ
nagai	SŌ	#	NŌ	SHIN	yashinau
r 168 s 8	mo	r 44 s 10	#	furueru..	r 184 s 15
	r 30 s 12		r 161 s 13	r 173 s 15	

口

占	古	舌	否	吉	告
divination; occupy	old, antiquated	tongue	negate	lucky	notify, announce
SEN	KO	ZETSU	HI	KICHI KITSU	KOKU
uranau shi+	furui..	shita	ina	#	tsugeru
r 25 s 5	r 30 s 5	r 135 s 6	r 30 s 7	r 30 s 6	r 30 s 7

合	谷	舍	含
unite; agree; fit	valley	building, house, hut	include, contain
GŌ GA' KA'	KOKU	SHA	GAN
au..	tani	#	fukumu..
r 30 s 6	r 150 s 7	r 9* s 8	r 30 s 7

台	名	各	召	君
pedestal; Taiwan	name; fame	each	summon	lord; you
DAI TAI	MEI MYŌ	KAKU	SHŌ	KUN
#	na	onoono	mesu	kimi
r 30* s 5	r 30 s 6	r 30 s 6	r 30 s 5	r 30 s 7

害	容	客	答	苦
harm	looks; contain	guest, customer	answer	pain; bitter
GAI	YŌ	KYAKU KAKU	TŌ	KU
#	#	#	kotae..	kurushii.. niga+
r 40 s 10	r 40 s 10	r 40 s 9	r 118 s 12	r 140 s 8

宮	営	善	喜
shrine, palace	management	good	rejoice
KYŪ GŪ KU	EI	ZEN	KI
miya	itonamu	yoi	yorokobu
r 40 s 10	r 30* s 12	r 30 s 12	r 30 s 12

啓	哲
enlighten	wisdom; philosophy
KEI	TETSU
#	#
r 30 s 11	r 30 s 10

言	誉	誓	警
say, speak; word	honor	vow	warn; police
GEN GON	YO	SEI	KEI
iu koto	homare	chikau	#
r 149 s 7	r 149 s 13	r 149 s 14	r 149 s 19

右	石	后	店	唐
right (hand)	stone	empress	shop, store	Cathay; *Tang*
U YŪ	SEKI SHAKU	KŌ	TEN	TŌ
migi	ishi	#	mise	Kara
r 30 s 5	r 112 s 5	r 30 s 6	r 53 s 8	r 30 s 10

若	岩	碁	磨	
young	rock, boulder	go (the board game)	polish	
JAKU NYAKU	GAN	GO	MA	
waka*i* mo+	iwa	#	miga*ku*	
r 140 s 8	r 46 s 8	r 112 s 13	r 112 s 16	

局	唇	居	倉
bureau; local; state, condition	lips	reside, be present	warehouse
KYOKU	SHIN	KYO	SŌ
#	kuchibiru	i*ru*	kura
r 44 s 7	r 30 s 10	r 44 s 8	r 9 s 10

可	司	句	奇	寄
possible; approve	official; officiate	phrase	strange	approach; give
KA	SHI	KU	KI	KI
#	#	#	#	yo*ru*..
r 30 s 5	r 30 s 5	r 30 s 5	r 37 s 8	r 40 s 11

尚	向	同	周	問	閣
facing	respect; valued	same	circumference	question	tower; cabinet
KŌ	SHŌ	DŌ	SHŪ	MON	KAKU
mu*kau*..	#	ona*ji*	mawa*ri*	to*i*.. ton	#
r 30 s 6	r 42 s 8	r 30 s 6	r 30 s 8	r 30 s 11	r 169 s 14

高	宮	官	管	筒	荷
high, tall; sum	shrine, palace	official; government	pipe; control	tube	load, cargo
KŌ	KYŪ GŪ KU	KAN	KAN	TŌ	KA
taka taka+	miya	#	kuda	tsutsu	ni
r 189 s 10	r 40 s 10	r 40 s 8	r 118 s 14	r 118 s 12	r 140 s 10

1	33
2	34
3	35
4	36
5	37
6	38
7	39
8	40
9	41
10	42
11	43
12	44
13	45
14	46
15	47
16	48
17	49
18	50
19	**51**
20	52
21	53
22	54
23	55
24	56
25	57
26	58
27	59
28	60
29	61
30	62
31	63
32	64

曰

旨	香	音	昔	普	曹
gist	fragrance	sound	ancient	universal	lawyer; companion
-	-	-	-	-	-
SHI	KŌ KYŌ	ON IN	SEKI SHAKU	FU	SŌ
mune	ka kao+	oto ne	mukashi		#
r 72 s 6	r 186 s 9	r 180 s 9	r 72 s 8	r 72 s 12	r 72* s 11

書	春	百	白
write; book	springtime	hundred	white
	-	-	-
SHO	SHUN	HYAKU	HAKU BYAKU
kaku	haru	#	shiroi shiro shira-
r 72* s 10	r 72 s 9	r 106 s 6	r 106 s 5

者	署	暑	暮	著
person	signature; (police) station	hot weather, summer	live; end; dusk	author; notable
-				
SHA	SHO	SHO	BO	CHO
mono	#	atsui	kureru..	arawasu ichijiru+
r 125 s 8	r 122 s 13	r 72 s 12	r 72 s 14	r 140 s 11

皆	習	替	暫	響
all	learn	exchange	temporary	echo
-	-	-	-	-
KAI	SHŪ	TAI	ZAN	KYŌ
mina	narau	kaeru..	#	hibiku
r 106 s 9	r 124 s 11	r 72* s 12	r 72 s 15	r 180 s 20

旬	暦	間	簡	層
10 day period	calendar	interval	simple, brief	layer
	-	-		
JUN	REKI	KAN KEN	KAN	SŌ
#	koyomi	aida ma	#	#
r 72 s 6	r 72 s 14	r 169 s 12	r 118 s 18	r 44 s 14

白

皆	習	百
all	learn	hundred
-	-	-
KAI	SHŪ	HYAKU
mina	narau	#
r 106 s 9	r 124 s 11	r 106 s 6

月

肖	育	肯	青	宵	背
resemble	bring up (child)	agreement	blue, green; young	dusk	back, rear; stature; defy
-		-		-	
SHŌ	IKU	KŌ	SEI SHŌ	SHŌ	HAI
#	sodateru..	#	ao ao+	yoi	se sei somo+
r 130 s 7	r 130 s 8	r 130 s 8	r 174 s 8	r 40 s 10	r 130 s 9

胃	骨	脅	有	肩	膚
stomach	bone	threaten	have; exist	shoulder	skin
I					
#	KOTSU	KYŌ	YŪ U	KEN	FU
	hone	obiyakasu odo+	aru	kata	#
r 130 s 9	r 188 s 10	r 130 s 10	r 130* s 6	r 130 s 8	r 130 s 15

田

苗	留	富			
seedling	detain	wealth			
-	-	-			
BYŌ	RYŪ RU	FU FŪ			
nae nawa	to*meru*..	tomi to+			
r 140　s 8	r 102　s 10	r 40　s 12			

雷	番	審	畜	蓄	奮
thunder	vigil; ranking	trial	livestock	amass	inspired, excited
-	-	-	-	-	-
RAI	BAN	SHIN	CHIKU	CHIKU	FUN
kaminari	#	#	#	takuwa*eru*	furu*u*
r 173　s 13	r 102　s 12	r 40　s 15	r 102　s 10	r 140　s 13	r 37　s 16

由	宙	笛	届
reason, cause	sky, (outer) space	flute	deliver
YU YŪ YUI	CHŪ	TEKI	#
yoshi	#	fue	todo*ku*..
r 102　s 5	r 40　s 8	r 118　s 11	r 44　s 8

由

宙	笛	届
sky, (outer) space	flute	deliver
CHŪ	TEKI	-
#	fue	#
r 40　s 8	r 118　s 11	todo*ku*..
		r 44　s 8

母

毎	毒
every, each	poison
MAI	DOKU
#	#
r 80　s 6	r 80　s 8

甼

竜	電
dragon	electricity
-	-
RYŪ	DEN
tatsu	#
r 117*　s 10	r 173　s 13

里

童	量	厘	重
child	quantity	*rin*	heavy; layered
DŌ	RYŌ	RIN	JŪ CHŌ
warabe	haka*ru*	#	omo*i* kasa+ -e
r 117　s 12	r 166　s 12	r 27　s 9	r 166　s 9

車

軍	輩	庫
army	fellow, companion	storehouse
-	-	-
GUN	HAI	KO KU
#	#	#
r 159　s 9	r 159　s 15	r 53　s 10

1	33
2	34
3	35
4	36
5	37
6	38
7	39
8	40
9	41
10	42
11	43
12	44
13	45
14	46
15	47
16	48
17	49
18	50
19	51
20	**52**
21	53
22	54
23	55
24	56
25	57
26	58
27	59
28	60
29	61
30	62
31	63
32	64

目 且 貝 見

目

首	盲	冒	省
head, neck; chief	blind	risk; defy	minister; omit; reflect upon; …
SHU	MŌ	BŌ	SHŌ SEI
kubi	-	okasu	habuku kaeri+
r 185 s 9	r 109 s 8	r 109* s 9	r 109 s 9

督	看	着	盾	自
supervise	watch over	arrive; wear, clothes	shield	oneself
TOKU	KAN	CHAKU JAKU	JUN	JI SHI
#	#	kiru.. tsu+	tate	mizukara
r 109 s 13	r 109 s 9	r 109* s 12	r 109 s 9	r 132 s 6

且

宜	査	畳
suitable; best wishes	investigate	fold up; *tatami* mat
GI	SA	JŌ
#	#	tatami tata+
r 40 s 8	r 75 s 9	r 102 s 12

貝

貞	負	貢	員	買
chastity	defeated; bear, suffer	tribute	member	buy
TEI	FU	KŌ KU	IN	BAI
#	makeru.. o+	mitsugu	#	kau
r 154 s 9	r 154 s 9	r 154 s 10	r 30 s 10	r 154 s 12

貴	貫	責	費	賞	賓
noble, valued	pierce; carry through	blame; duty	cost	prize	guest
KI	KAN	SEKI	HI	SHŌ	HIN
tattoi.. tōto+	tsuranuku	semeru	tsuiyasu..	#	#
r 154 s 12	r 154 s 11	r 154 s 11	r 154 s 12	r 154 s 15	r 154 s 15

貧	貨	貸	賃	資
poverty	goods; coin, money	lend, rent out	fee, wages	assets
HIN BIN	KA	TAI	CHIN	SHI
mazushii	#	kasu	#	#
r 154 s 11	r 154 s 11	r 154 s 12	r 154 s 13	r 154 s 13

賛	賀	貿	賢	質
praise, approve	good wishes	trade	wise	quality; hostage
SAN	GA	BŌ	KEN	SHITSU SHICHI CHI
#	#	#	kashikoi	#
r 154 s 15	r 154 s 12	r 154 s 12	r 154 s 16	r 154 s 15

見

覚	寛	覧
memorize; awake	tolerant	look at
KAKU	KAN	RAN
oboeru sa+	#	#
r 147 s 12	r 40 s 13	r 147 s 17

石

岩	碁	磨	若
rock, boulder	go (the board game)	polish	young
GAN	GO	-	-
iwa	#	MA	JAKU NYAKU
r 46 s 8	r 112 s 13	miga*ku*	waka*i* mo+
		r 112 s 16	r 140 s 8

皿

益	盆	盛	血
benefit	tray	prosperous; heap up	blood
-	-	SEI JŌ	-
EKI YAKU	BON	saka*ru*.. mo+	KETSU
#	#	r 108 s 11	chi
r 108 s 10	r 108 s 9		r 143 s 6

盗	盟	監	盤
steal	alliance	oversee	disk; tray, board, base
-	-	-	BAN
TŌ	MEI	KAN	#
nusu*mu*	#	#	r 108 s 15
r 108 s 11	r 108 s 13	r 108 s 15	

口

器
container; utensil; skill
KI
utsuwa
r 30 s 15

語	詔	話	詰	諾	諮
language, word; talk	imperial edict	speak; tale	cram; rebuke	consent	consult
GO	SHŌ	WA	KITSU	-	-
kata*ru*..	mikotonori	hanashi hana+	tsu*mu*..	DAKU	SHI
r 149 s 14	r 149 s 12	r 149 s 13	r 149 s 13	#	haka*ru*
				r 149 s 15	r 149 s 16

虫

蛍	蛮	蚕	風
firefly	barbarian	silkworm	wind; style
-	-	-	FŪ FU
KEI	BAN	SAN	kaze kaza-
hotaru	#	kaiko	r 182 s 9
r 142 s 11	r 142 s 12	r 142 s 10	

言

誉	誓	警
honor	vow	warn; police
-	-	KEI
YO	SEI	#
homa*re*	chika*u*	r 149 s 19
r 149 s 13	r 149 s 14	

	策 plan, policy / SAKU / # / r118 s12	筆 writing brush / HITSU / fude / r118 s12	奔 hurry / - / HON / # / r37 s8	星 star / - / SEI SHŌ / hoshi / r72 s9	産 give birth / - / SAN / ubu u+ / r100 s11
束 聿 卉 生					
∟ 丰 氺	亡 deceased / - / BŌ MŌ / nai / r8 s3	奉 offering; respectful / HŌ BU / tatematsuru / r37 s8	半 half, semi-, pen- / HAN / nakaba / r24 s5	暴 violent / - / BŌ BAKU / abareru.. / r72 s15	泰 tranquil / - / TAI / # / r85 s10
之 立 少 良	芝 turf / # / shiba / r140 s6	翌 next / YOKU / # / r124 s11	歩 walk / HO BU FU / aruku ayu+ / r77 s8	養 foster, rear / YŌ / yashinau / r184 s15	
月 尸 𠀎 人	斉 equal / - / SEI / # / r67* s8	斎 purify; abstain from / SAI / # / r67* s11	粛 solemn; purge / SHUKU / # / r129 s11	肉 meat, flesh / NIKU / # / r130 s6	腐 rot / - / FU / kusaru.. / r130 s14
九 午 友 方	究 research, investigate / KYŪ / kiwameru / r116 s7	卑 lowly / - / HI / iyashii.. / r24 s9	髪 hair / - / HATSU / kami / r190 s14	芳 fragrant; (honorific) your / HŌ / kanbashii / r140 s7	房 room; tassel / BŌ / fusa / r63 s8
夕 勿 乡	多 many / - / TA / ōi / r36 s6	夢 dream / - / MU / yume / r36 s13	易 easy; trade; divination / EKI I / yasashii / r72 s8	参 visit; join in / SAN / mairu / r28 s8	
ㄅ 升 我 食	考 consider / - / KŌ / kangaeru / r125 s6	昇 rise / - / SHŌ / noboru / r72 s8	義 righteous; meaning; ... / GI / # / r123 s13	養 foster, rear / YŌ / yashinau / r184 s15	
介 今 令 分	界 world; scope / KAI / # / r102 s9	琴 harp / KIN / koto / r96 s12	零 zero / REI / # / r173 s13	雰 atmosphere / FUN / # / r173 s12	

号	**需**	**矛**	**発**	
number, designation	need, demand	spear, lance	emit; start	
GŌ	JU	MU	HATSU HOTSU	
#	#	hoko	#	
r 30* s 5	r 173 s 14	r 110 s 5	r 105 s 9	
並	**霊**	**整**	**症**	
line up; ordinary	spirit, soul	arrange	symptoms	
HEI	REI RYŌ	SEI	SHŌ	
narabu.. nami	tama	sadameru..	#	
r 1* s 8	r 173 s 15	r 66 s 16	r 104 s 10	
宝	**璽**	**登**	**豊**	**痘**
treasure	imperial seal	climb	abundant	smallpox
HŌ	JI	TŌ TO	HŌ	TŌ
takara	#	noboru	yutaka	#
r 40 s 8	r 96 s 19	r 105 s 12	r 151 s 13	r 104 s 12
定	**是**	**奏**	**笑**	**宅**
fix, decide	right, just; this	play music	laugh	home
TEI JŌ	ZE	SŌ	SHŌ	TAKU
totonoeru..	#	kanaderu	warau e+	#
r 40 s 8	r 72 s 9	r 37 s 9	r 118 s 10	r 40 s 6
当	**雪**	**今**	**琴**	**秀**
hit; this; applicable	snow	now	harp	excellent
TŌ	SETSU	KIN KON	KIN	SHŪ
ateru..	yuki	ima	koto	hiideru
r 58* s 6	r 173 s 11	r 9 s 4	r 96 s 12	r 115 s 7
令	**零**	**第**	**厄**	**危**
orders	zero	Number (as in 'Number 3')	misfortune	dangerous
REI	REI	DAI	YAKU	KI
#	#	#	#	abunai aya+
r 9 s 5	r 173 s 13	r 118 s 11	r 27 s 4	r 26 s 6
巻	**包**	**官**	**管**	**虐**
roll; scroll; book	wrap	official; government	pipe; control	cruel
KAN	HŌ	KAN	KAN	GYAKU
maki ma+	tsutsumu	#	kuda	shiitageru
r 49* s 9	r 20 s 5	r 40 s 8	r 118 s 14	r 141 s 9
甚	**農**	**震**	**篤**	**驚**
extremely	farming	quake	good; seriously	surprise
JIN	NŌ	SHIN	TOKU	KYŌ
hanahada..	#	furueru..	#	odoroku..
r 99 s 9	r 161 s 13	r 173 s 15	r 118 s 16	r 187 s 22

万 而 才 无

亚 正

玉 豆

王 夭 毛

日 乃

弔 巴

目 臣

辰 馬

厂

圧	反	厄	灰	原	厚
pressure	oppose; bend, warp	misfortune	ash	prairie; origin	thick; cordial
-	HAN HON TAN	-	-	GEN	KŌ
ATSU	so*ru*..	YAKU	KAI	hara	atsu*i*
#		#	hai		
r 32 s 5	r 29 s 4	r 27 s 4	r 86 s 6	r 27 s 10	r 27 s 9

厘	暦	歴	唇	辱	
rin	calendar	history, career, CV.	lips	disgrace, insult	
-	-	REKI	-	JOKU	
RIN	REKI	#	SHIN	hazukashi*meru*	
#	koyomi		kuchibiru		
r 27 s 9	r 72 s 14	r 77 s 14	r 30 s 10	r 161 s 10	

励	石				
encourage; diligent	stone				
REI	-				
hage*mu*..	SEKI SHAKU				
r 19 s 7	ishi				
	r 112 s 5				

厂

斤	斥	后	盾	丘	氏
kin	repel	empress	shield	hill	family name
-	-	-	-	KYŪ	SHI
KIN	SEKI	KŌ	JUN	oka	uji
#	#	#	tate		
r 69 s 4	r 69 s 5	r 30 s 6	r 109 s 9	r 1 s 5	r 83 s 4

ナ

左	右	友	布	有	石
left (hand)	right (hand)	friend	cloth; spread	have; exist	stone
SA	U YŪ	-	FU	YŪ U	-
hidari	migi	YŪ	nuno	a*ru*	SEKI SHAKU
		tomo			ishi
r 48 s 5	r 30 s 5	r 29 s 4	r 50 s 5	r 130* s 6	r 112 s 5

オ

在	存
be located; exist; suburbs	exist; think that
ZAI	SON ZON
a*ru*	#
r 32 s 6	r 39 s 6

庁 government agency CHŌ # r53 s5	広 wide - KŌ hiro*i..* r53 s5	床 bed; floor SHŌ toko yuka r53 s7	応 respond - Ō # r61 s7	店 shop, store TEN mise r53 s8	序 preface; rank, order JO # r53 s7
底 bottom, base TEI soko r53 s8	座 sit, seat ZA suwa*ru* r53 s10	庶 multitude - SHO # r53 s11	度 degree, extent; times; … DO TAKU TO tabi r53 s9	席 seat, place SEKI # r50 s10	唐 Cathay; *Tang* TŌ Kara r30 s10
庫 storehouse - KO KU # r53 s10	廉 honest; cheap REN # r53 s13	康 healthy; safe KŌ # r53 s11	庸 ordinary - YŌ # r53 s11	皮 skin - HI kawa r107 s5	
府 metropolis; government FU # r53 s8	麻 hemp; numb MA asa r200 s11	廊 corridor - RŌ # r53 s12	庭 garden - TEI niwa r53 s10	応 respond - Ō # r61 s7	
廃 obsolete, waste, scrap HAI sutare*ru..* r53 s12	磨 polish - MA miga*ku* r112 s16	摩 rub - MA # r64 s15	魔 demon, devil MA # r194 s21	腐 rot - FU kusa*ru..* r130 s14	慶 celebrate - KEI # r61 s15
症 symptoms - SHŌ # r104 s10	疾 disease; speed - SHITSU # r104 s10	疲 fatigue - HI tsuka*reru..* r104 s10	病 illness - BYŌ HEI yamai ya+ r104 s9	疫 epidemic - EKI YAKU # r104 s9	痘 smallpox - TŌ # r104 s12
痛 pain - TSŪ ita*mu..* r104 s12	痢 diarrhea - RI # r104 s12	痴 foolish - CHI # r104 s13	癖 habit - HEKI kuse r104 s18	癒 heal - YU # r104 s18	療 treat illness - RYŌ # r104 s17
虐 cruel - GYAKU shiita*geru* r141 s9	虚 void - KYO KO # r141 s11	慮 consider; concern for - RYO # r61 s15	虜 captive - RYO # r141 s13	虞 anxiety - # osore r141 s13	膚 skin - FU # r130 s15

尸 尸 戸 耂 方

尸

尺	尽	昼	尼	尾	尿
shaku; measure	exhaust	daytime, noon	nun	tail	urine
SHAKU	-	CHŪ	NI	BI	NYŌ
#	JIN	hiru	ama	o	#
	tsuku*su*..				
r44 s4	r44* s6	r72 s9	r44 s5	r44 s7	r44 s7

届	屈	局
deliver	bend; yield	bureau; local; state, condition
-	KUTSU	KYOKU
#	#	#
todo*ku*..		
r44 s8	r44 s8	r44 s7

居	屋	展	属	層	履
reside, be present	house; -seller	display, unfold	belong	layer	shoes; do
KYO	OKU	TEN	-	-	RI
i*ru*	ya	#	ZOKU	SŌ	ha*ku*
r44 s8	r44 s9	r44 s10	r44 s12	r44 s14	r44 s15

民	刷	尉	殿
the people	print	military officer	Mr, Mrs; palace
-	-	I	DEN TEN
MIN	SATSU	#	tono -dono
tami	su*ru*		
r83 s5	r18 s8	r41 s11	r79 s13

戸

戻	房	肩	扇	扉	雇
return	room; tassel	shoulder	fan (folding, electric)	door	employ
-	BŌ	-	SEN	-	-
REI	fusa	KEN	ōgi	HI	KO
modo*ru*..		kata		tobira	yato*u*
r63 s7	r63 s8	r130 s8	r63 s10	r63 s12	r172 s12

戸
door
-
KO
to
r63 s4

耂

老	考	孝	者	煮
old age	consider	filial piety	person	boil, cook
RŌ	KŌ	KŌ	SHA	SHA
o*iru* fu+	kanga*eru*	#	mono	ni*eru*..
r125 s6	r125 s6	r39 s7	r125 s8	r86 s12

方

放	旅	施	旋	族	旗
set free; emit	travel	do; donate	rotation	family	flag
HŌ	RYO	SHI SE	SEN	ZOKU	KI
hana*tsu*..	tabi	hodoku*su*	#	#	hata
r66 s8	r70 s10	r70 s9	r70 s11	r70 s11	r70 s14

■

ナ 歹 尸

十 产 产

⺍ 羊

三 手

ク 尹

一 咠 仐

石	死	后
stone	death	empress
-	-	-
SEKI SHAKU	SHI	KŌ
ishi	shi*nu*	#
r 112 s 5	r 78 s 6	r 30 s 6
皮	危	産
skin	dangerous	give birth
-	-	-
HI	KI	SAN
kawa	abu*nai* aya+	ubu u+
r 107 s 5	r 26 s 6	r 100 s 11
厳	差	着
severe	difference	arrive; wear, clothes
GEN GON	SA	CHAKU JAKU
kibi*shii* ogoso+	sa*su*	ki*ru*.. tsu+
r 27* s 17	r 48 s 10	r 109* s 12
寿	看	
longevity	watch over	
-	-	
JU	KAN	
kotobuki	#	
r 41* s 7	r 109 s 9	
名	多	君
name; fame	many	lord; you
MEI MYŌ	TA	KUN
na	ō*i*	kimi
r 30 s 6	r 36 s 6	r 30 s 7
取	最	倉
take	utmost	warehouse
-	-	-
SHU	SAI	SŌ
to*ru*	motto*mo*	kura
r 29 s 8	r 72* s 12	r 9 s 10

1	33
2	34
3	35
4	36
5	37
6	38
7	39
8	40
9	41
10	42
11	43
12	44
13	45
14	46
15	47
16	48
17	49
18	50
19	51
20	52
21	53
22	54
23	55
24	**56**
25	57
26	58
27	59
28	60
29	61
30	62
31	63
32	64

迺

迭	速	連	逮	進
take turns	quick	linked; series	capture	advance
-	-	REN	-	-
TETSU	SOKU	tsu*reru* tsura+	TAI	SHIN
#	haya*i*.. sumi+		#	susu*mu*..
r 162 s 8	r 162 s 10	r 162 s 10	r 162 s 11	r 162 s 11

込	辺	逐	退	遇
crowded; enter, insert	vicinity	expel; in turn	retreat	meet; deal with
#	HEN	CHIKU	TAI	GŪ
ko*mu*..	atari -be	#	shirizo*ku*..	#
r 162 s 5	r 162 s 5	r 162 s 10	r 162 s 9	r 162 s 12

述	迷	迫	追
say	astray, lost	press, urge; approach	chase; expel
-	-	-	-
JUTSU	MEI	HAKU	TSUI
no*beru*	mayo*u*	sema*ru*	o*u*
r 162 s 8	r 162 s 9	r 162 s 8	r 162 s 9

迎

迎	逃	進
welcome	escape	advance
-	-	-
GEI	TŌ	SHIN
muka*eru*	ni*geru*.. noga+	susu*mu*..
r 162 s 7	r 162 s 9	r 162 s 11

逝	避	遊	巡
die, death	evade	fun, play; tour	patrol, tour
SEI	HI	YŪ YU	JUN
yu*ku*	sa*keru*	aso*bu*	megu*ru*
r 162 s 10	r 162 s 16	r 162 s 12	r 47 s 6

迺

近	返	遮	遍	遅	逓
near; recent	return, repay	obstruct	widespread	slow; delayed	relay; in turn
KIN	HEN	-	-	CHI	TEI
chika*i*	kae*ru*..	SHA	HEN	oso*i* oku+	#
r 162 s 7	r 162 s 7	saegi*ru*	#	r 162 s 12	r 162 s 10
		r 162 s 14	r 162 s 12		

迺

迅
quick
-
JIN
#
r 162 s 6

迺

週	過	適
week	exceed; err	suitable
-	-	-
SHŪ	KA	TEKI
#	su*giru*.. ayama+	#
r 162 s 11	r 162 s 12	r 162 s 14

迫
press, urge;
approach
HAKU
sema*ru*
r 162 s 8

追
chase;
expel
TSUI
o*u*
r 162 s 9

述
say
-
JUTSU
no*beru*
r 162 s 8

迷
astray,
lost
MEI
mayo*u*
r 162 s 9

送
send
-
SŌ
oku*ru*
r 162 s 9

逆
inverse;
counter-
GYAKU
saka saka+
r 162 s 9

遂
accomplish
-
SUI
to*geru*
r 162 s 12

道
way,
road
DŌ TŌ
michi
r 162 s 12

遵
comply
-
JUN
#
r 162 s 15

造
make
-
ZŌ
tsuku*ru*
r 162 s 10

遺
bequeath
-
I YUI
#
r 162 s 15

遣
send;
spend; use
KEN
tsuka*u..*
r 162 s 13

違
differ;
disobey
I
chiga*u..*
r 162 s 13

遠
distant
-
EN ON
tō*i*
r 162 s 13

達
achieve
-
TATSU
#
r 162 s 12

適
suitable
-
TEKI
#
r 162 s 14

逮
capture
-
TAI
#
r 162 s 11

遭
encounter
-
SŌ
a*u*
r 162 s 14

逸
miss, let slip;
deviate; excel
ITSU
#
r 162 s 11

途
way
-
TO
#
r 162 s 10

透
transparent
-
TŌ
su*ku..*
r 162 s 10

遍
widespread
-
HEN
#
r 162 s 12

遷
transition
-
SEN
#
r 162 s 15

還
return
-
KAN
#
r 162 s 16

運
transport;
luck
UN
hako*bu*
r 162 s 12

通
pass; street;
commute; ...
TSŪ TSU
tō*ru..* kayo+
r 162 s 10

選
select
-
SEN
era*bu*
r 162 s 15

導
guide
-
DŌ
michibi*ku*
r 41 s 15

廴 走

廴

廷
law court
-
TEI
#
r 54　s 7

延
prolong;
postpone
-
EN
no*basu*..
r 54　s 8

建
build
-
KEN KON
ta*teru*..
r 54　s 9

走

赴
go to
-
FU
omomu*ku*
r 156　s 9

起
wake up,
rise; begin
-
KI
o*kiru*..
r 156　s 10

超
surpass
-
CHŌ
ko*su*..
r 156　s 12

趣
gist; motive;
elegance
-
SHU
omomuki
r 156　s 15

越
exceed
-
ETSU
ko*su*..
r 156　s 12

■

左

是

鬼

直	置	断	県
directly; fix	put, place	sever; decide	prefecture
CHOKU JIKI	- CHI	- DAN	- KEN
nao*su*.. tada+	o*ku*	kotowa*ru* ta+	#
r 109 s 8	r 122 s 13	r 69 s 11	r 109* s 9

処	題
deal with	title, topic
- SHO	DAI
#	#
r 16* s 5	r 181 s 18

勉	魅
diligent; strive	enchant
BEN	- MI
#	#
r 19 s 10	r 194 s 15

寸	可	司	奇	寄
tiny	possible; approve	official; officiate	strange	approach; give
-			-	
SUN	KA	SHI	KI	KI
#	#	#	#	yo*ru*..
r 41 s 3	r 30 s 5	r 30 s 5	r 37 s 8	r 40 s 11

勺	句	旬	包	匁
shaku	phrase	10 day period	wrap	*monme*
SHAKU	KU	JUN	HŌ	
#	#	#	tsutsu*mu*	#
r 20 s 3	r 30 s 5	r 72 s 6	r 20 s 5	monme r 20 s 4

式	弐	武	戒	我
rite; style	two	military	warn; command	I, my; self; selfish
SHIKI	NI	BU MU	KAI	GA
#	#	#	imashi*meru*	ware wa
r 56 s 6	r 56* s 6	r 77 s 8	r 62 s 7	r 62 s 7

成	威	栽	載	裁	幾
become; consist of	power; threat	plant	load; publish	judge; cut	how many
SEI JŌ	I	SAI	SAI	SAI	KI
na*ru*..	#	#	no*ru*..	saba*ku* ta+	iku
r 62 s 6	r 38 s 9	r 75 s 10	r 159 s 13	r 145 s 12	r 52 s 12

飛	鳥	島
fly, jump	bird	island
HI	CHŌ	TŌ
to*bu*..	tori	shima
r 183 s 9	r 196 s 11	r 46 s 10

斗	以	少
ladle;	by means of; datum	few
to		-
TO	I	SHŌ
#	#	suko*shi* suku+
r 68 s 4	r 9 s 5	r 42 s 4

区
district,
ward
KU
#
r 22* s 4

匹
comparable
-
HITSU
hiki
r 22* s 4

巨
huge
-
KYO
#
r 48 s 5

臣
vassal,
retainer
SHIN JIN
#
r 131 s 7

医
doctor;
medical
I
#
r 22* s 7

匠
craftsman
-
SHŌ
#
r 22 s 6

匿
conceal
-
TOKU
#
r 22* s 10

枢
pivotal
-
SŪ
#
r 75 s 8

駆
spur on;
drive; expel
KU
ka*ru*..
r 187 s 14

冠
crown
-
KAN
kanmuri
r 14 s 9

鬼
demon;
ghost
KI
oni
r 194 s 10

凶
misfortune;
evil
KYŌ
#
r 17 s 4

山
mountain
-
SAN
yama
r 46 s 3

出
go out, exit;
put out
SHUTSU SUI
de*ru* da+
r 17 s 5

画
picture;
kanji stroke
GA KAKU
#
r 102 s 8

幽
deep; hidden;
remote; …
YŪ
#
r 52 s 9

歯
tooth
-
SHI
ha
r 77* s 12

凹
concave,
hollow
-
Ō
#
r 17 s 5

凸
concave
-
TOTSU
#
r 17 s 5

冂 刀 几 門

冂
刀
几
門

同	円	内	肉	向	尚
same	circle;	inside	meat,	facing	respect;
-	yen	-	flesh	-	valued
DŌ	EN	NAI DAI	NIKU	KŌ	SHŌ
onaji	marui	uchi	#	mukau..	#
r 30 s 6	r 13* s 4	r 13* s 4	r 130 s 6	r 30 s 6	r 42 s 8

周	丹	舟	用	月	
circum-	vermilion;	boat	task; use,	month; moon;	
ference	sincerely	-	employ	Monday	
SHŪ	TAN	SHŪ	YŌ	GETSU GATSU	
mawari	#	fune funa-	mochiiru	tsuki	
r 30 s 8	r 3 s 4	r 137 s 6	r 101 s 5	r 74 s 4	

凡	風				
ordinary	wind;				
-	style				
BON HAN	FŪ FU				
#	kaze kaza-				
r 16 s 3	r 182 s 9				

問	間	聞	閑	閉	開
question	interval	hear, listen;	leisure	closed	open
-	-	ask	-	-	-
MON	KAN KEN	BUN MON	KAN	HEI	KAI
toi.. ton	aida ma	kiku..	#	shimeru.. to+	akeru.. hira+
r 30 s 11	r 169 s 12	r 128 s 14	r 169 s 12	r 169 s 11	r 169 s 12

関	閲	閣	閥	闘	
barrier;	review	tower;	clique	fight	
connected	-	cabinet	-	-	
KAN	ETSU	KAKU	BATSU	TŌ	
seki	#	#	#	tatakau	
r 169 s 14	r 169 s 15	r 169 s 14	r 169 s 14	r 169* s 18	

簡	門				
simple,	gate,				
brief	door				
KAN	MON				
#	kado				
r 118 s 18	r 169 s 8				

券	巻
ticket	roll; scroll; book
-	-
KEN	KAN
#	maki ma+
r 18 s 8	r 49* s 9

奉	春	奏	泰
offering; respectful	springtime	play music	tranquil
HŌ BU	SHUN	SŌ	TAI
tatematsuru	haru	kanaderu	#
r 37 s 8	r 72 s 9	r 37 s 9	r 85 s 10

太	冬	寒	寿	為	参
thick; great	winter	cold	longevity	do; purpose	visit; join in
TA TAI	TŌ	KAN	JU	I	SAN
futoi..	fuyu	samui	kotobuki	#	mairu
r 37 s 4	r 15* s 5	r 40 s 12	r 41* s 7	r 86* s 9	r 28 s 8

尽	昼	局
exhaust	daytime, noon	bureau; local; state, condition
-	-	-
JIN	CHŪ	KYOKU
tsukusu..	hiru	#
r 44* s 6	r 72 s 9	r 44 s 7

威	蔵	繭	雨
power; threat	store, keep	cocoon	rain
I	ZŌ	KEN	U
#	kura	mayu	ame ama-
r 38 s 9	r 140 s 15	r 120 s 18	r 173 s 8

何	伺	河	筒	荷
what, how many	visit; pay respects	river	tube	load, cargo
KA	SHI	KA	TŌ	KA
nani nan	ukagau	kawa	tsutsu	ni
r 9 s 7	r 9 s 7	r 85 s 8	r 118 s 12	r 140 s 10

高	商	南
high, tall; sum	trade	south
KŌ	SHŌ	NAN NA
taka taka+	akinau	minami
r 189 s 10	r 30 s 11	r 24 s 9

囚	因	困	田	四
prisoner	cause	suffer; trouble	rice field	four
-	-	KON	-	-
SHŪ	IN	komaru	DEN	SHI
#	yoru		ta	yo yo+ yo¹+ yon
r 31　s 5	r 31　s 6	r 31　s 7	r 102　s 5	r 31　s 5

回	団	図	囲	国
turn, rotate; times	.group, body	diagram	encircle	country
KAI E	DAN TON	ZU TO	-	-
mawasu	#	hakaru	I	KOKU
r 31　s 6	r 31　s 6	r 31　s 7	kakomu..	kuni
			r 31　s 7	r 31　s 8

固	園	圏
firm, hard	gardens	sphere
KO	-	-
katai..	EN	KEN
r 31　s 8	sono	#
	r 31　s 13	r 31　s 12

口	日	目
mouth	day; Japan; sun; Sunday	eye; -th
-	NICHI JITSU	-
KŌ KU	hi -ka	MOKU BOKU
kuchi	r 72　s 4	me ma-
r 30　s 3		r 109　s 5

丹	舟	母	箇	菌
vermilion; sincerely	boat	mother	item	germ; fungi
TAN	-	-	-	KIN
#	SHŪ	BO	KA	#
r 3　s 4	fune funa-	haha	#	r 140　s 11
	r 137　s 6	r 80　s 5	r 118　s 14	

術	街	衝	衛	衡	
art, skill	street, arcade	collide	guard	balance, scales	
-	GAI KAI	-	-	-	
JUTSU	machi	SHŌ	EI	KŌ	
#	#	#	#	#	
r 60* s 11	r 60* s 12	r 60* s 15	r 60* s 16	r 60* s 16	

問	間	聞	閑	閉	開
question	interval	hear, listen; ask	leisure	closed	open
-	-	-	-	-	-
MON	KAN KEN	BUN MON	KAN	HEI	KAI
to*i.. ton*	aida ma	ki*ku..	#	shi*meru.. to+*	a*keru.. hira+*
r 30 s 11	r 169 s 12	r 128 s 14	r 169 s 12	r 169 s 11	r 169 s 12

関	閲	閣	閥	闘	
barrier; connected	review	tower; cabinet	clique	fight	
KAN	ETSU	KAKU	BATSU	TŌ	
seki	#	#	#	tataka*u	
r 169 s 14	r 169 s 15	r 169 s 14	r 169 s 14	r 169* s 18	

班	承	門	簡	行
squad	consent; be told	gate, door	simple, brief	go; do; line
-	-	-	-	-
HAN	SHŌ	MON	KAN	GYŌ KŌ AN
#	uketamawa*ru	kado	#	i*ku yu+ okona+
r 96 s 10	r 64 s 8	r 169 s 8	r 118 s 18	r 144 s 6

疑	務	能	殺	
doubt	duties	ability; *Noh* play	kill	
-	-	NŌ	SATSU SETSU SAI	
GI	MU	#	koro*su	
utaga*u	tsuto*meru			
r 103 s 14	r 19 s 11	r 130 s 10	r 79 s 10	

競	鼓	殻	穀	行
compete	drum	shell	grain, cereal	go; do; line
-	-	-	KOKU	-
KYŌ KEI	KO	KAKU	#	GYŌ KŌ AN
kiso*u se+	tsuzumi	kara		i*ku yu+ okona+
r 117 s 20	r 207 s 13	r 79 s 11	r 115 s 14	r 144 s 6

辞	韻	静	解	齢
word; resign	rhyme, tone	quiet	unravel; solve	age
JI	IN	-	KAI GE	-
ya*meru	#	SEI JŌ	to*ku..	REI
r 160 s 13	r 180 s 19	shizu shizu+		#
		r 174 s 14	r 148 s 13	r 211 s 17

For ⊞ see also 言 on page 14 and ⺾ on page 41.

1	33
2	34
3	35
4	36
5	37
6	38
7	39
8	40
9	41
10	42
11	43
12	44
13	45
14	46
15	47
16	48
17	49
18	50
19	51
20	52
21	53
22	54
23	55
24	56
25	57
26	58
27	59
28	60
29	**61**
30	62
31	63
32	64

十	土	士	止	上
ten	soil, land;	warrior;	stop	above,
-	Saturday	man	-	up
JŪ JI'	DO TO	SHI	SHI	JŌ SHŌ
tō to	tsuchi	#	to*maru*..	ue kami uwa- a+ nobo+
r 24 s 2	r 32 s 3	r 33 s 3	r 77 s 4	r 1 s 3

山	出	屯	亡	七
mountain	go out, exit;	barracks	deceased	seven
-	put out	-	-	
SAN	SHUTSU SUI	TON	BŌ MŌ	SHICHI
yama	de*ru* da+	#	na*i*	nana nana+ nano
r 46 s 3	r 17 s 5	r 45 s 4	r 8 s 3	r 1 s 2

木	本	米	来	未	末
tree, wood;	book; this;	rice;	come	not yet	end
Thursday	base	America	-	-	
BOKU MOKU	HON	BEI MAI	RAI	MI	MATSU BATSU
ki ko-	moto	kome	ku*ru* kita+	#	sue
r 75 s 4	r 75 s 5	r 119 s 6	r 75* s 7	r 75 s 5	r 75 s 5

半	牛	朱	生
half,	cow, bull	vermilion	life; birth;
semi-, pen-	-	-	grow; raw
HAN	GYŪ	SHU	SHŌ SEI
naka*ba*	ushi	#	nama i+ u+ ha+ o+ ki-
r 24 s 5	r 93 s 4	r 75 s 6	r 100 s 5

斗	寸	才	与	皮	衣
ladle;	tiny	talent;	give	skin	garment
to	-	years old	-	-	-
TO	SUN	SAI	YO	HI	I
#	#	#	ata*eru*	kawa	koromo
r 68 s 4	r 41 s 3	r 64 s 3	r 1* s 3	r 107 s 5	r 145 s 6

小	水	氷	永	求
small	water;	ice	eternal	seek,
-	Wednesday	-	-	request
SHŌ	SUI	HYŌ	EI	KYŪ
chii*sai* ko- o-	mizu	kōri kō- hi	naga*i*	moto*meru*
r 42 s 3	r 85 s 4	r 85 s 5	r 85 s 5	r 85 s 7

中	虫	束	事	肅
middle;	insect	bundle	thing,	solemn;
China	-	-	matter	purge
CHŪ	CHŪ	SOKU	JI ZU	SHUKU
naka	mushi	taba	koto	#
r 2 s 4	r 142 s 6	r 75 s 7	r 6 s 8	r 129 s 11

申	由	東	車
say,	reason,	east	vehicle
report	cause	-	-
SHIN	YU YŪ YUI	TŌ	SHA
mō*su*	yoshi	higashi	kuruma
r 102 s 5	r 102 s 5	r 75 s 8	r 159 s 7

止	片	甘	井	世	曲
stop	part, flake; single, one-	sweet	well (for water)	world; era	bend; melody
-	HEN	-	SEI SHŌ	SE SEI	KYOKU
SHI	kata	KAN	i	yo	ma*geru*..
to*maru*..	r 91 s 4	ama*i*..	r 7 s 4	r 1 s 5	r 72* s 6
r 77 s 4		r 99 s 5			

甚
extremely
-
JIN
hanaha*da*..
r 99 s 9

人	火	入	八
person	fire; Tuesday	enter; put in, let in	eight
-	KA	NYŪ	HACHI
JIN NIN	hi ho	hai*ru* i+	ya ya'+ ya+ yō
hito	r 86 s 4	r 11 s 2	r 12 s 2
r 9 s 2			

大	犬	太	夫	失	先
large	dog	thick; great	husband	lose; error	ahead; previous
-	-	TA TAI	FU FŪ	SHITSU	SEN
DAI TAI	KEN	futo*i*..	otto	ushina*u*	saki
ō- ō+	inu	r 37 s 4	r 37 s 4	r 37 s 5	r 10 s 6
r 37 s 3	r 94 s 4				

丈	史	吏	央
robust; height, stature	history	official	center
JŌ	-	-	-
take	SHI	RI	Ō
r 1 s 3	#	#	#
	r 30 s 5	r 30 s 6	r 37 s 5

内	肉	力	丸	九
inside	meat, flesh	power	round	nine
-	NIKU	-	-	KYŪ KU
NAI DAI	#	RIKI RYOKU	GAN	kokono kokono+
uchi	r 130 s 6	chikara	-maru maru+	r 5 s 2
r 13* s 4		r 19 s 2	r 3 s 3	

女	与	糸	寿
woman	give	thread	longevity
-	-	-	-
JO NYO NYŌ	YO	SHI	JU
onna me	ata*eru*	ito	kotobuki
r 38 s 3	r 1* s 3	r 120 s 6	r 41* s 7

一
one
-
ICHI ITSU
hito*tsu* hito-
r 1 s 1

丁
city block;
4th; ...
CHŌ TEI
#
r 1 s 2

工
industry;
worker
KŌ KU
#
r 48 s 3

不
not,
un-
FU BU
#
r 1 s 4

下
below,
down
KA GE
shita moto shimo sa+ o+ kuda+
r 1 s 3

干
dry
-
KAN
hi*ru* ho+
r 51 s 3

平
level;
calm
HEI BYŌ
hira tai+
r 51 s 5

王
king
-
Ō
#
r 96 s 4

玉
jewel
-
GYOKU
tama
r 96 s 5

正
correct
-
SHŌ SEI
tada*su*.. masa
r 77 s 5

五
five
-
GO
itsu itsu+
r 7 s 4

天
heaven,
sky
TEN
ame ama-
r 37 s 4

万
ten thousand;
many
MAN BAN
#
r 1* s 3

石
stone
-
SEKI SHAKU
ishi
r 112 s 5

死
death
-
SHI
shi*nu*
r 78 s 6

互
mutual
-
GO
taga*i*
r 7 s 4

丙
3rd
-
HEI
#
r 1 s 5

両
both
-
RYŌ
#
r 1* s 6

雨
rain
-
U
ame ama-
r 173 s 8

西
west
-
SEI SAI
nishi
r 146 s 6

亜
Asia;
sub-
A
#
r 7 s 7

耳
ear
-
JI
mimi
r 128 s 6

更
renew;
late
KŌ
sara fu+
r 72* s 7

再
again;
re-
SAI SA
futata*bi*
r 13 s 6

画
picture;
kanji stroke
GA KAKU
#
r 102* s 8

百
hundred
-
HYAKU
#
r 106 s 6

面
face,
mask
MEN
omote omo tsura
r 176 s 9

Kanji	Meaning		Readings	Radical/Strokes
巨	huge	-	KYO / #	r 48 s 5
臣	vassal, retainer	-	SHIN JIN / #	r 131 s 7
匹	comparable	-	HITSU / hiki	r 22* s 4
民	the people	-	MIN / tami	r 83 s 5
長	long; chief	-	CHŌ / naga*i*	r 168 s 8
馬	horse	-	BA / uma ma	r 187 s 10
又	again	-	# / mata	r 29 s 2
乙	2nd	-	OTSU / #	r 5 s 1
己	self	-	KI KO / onore	r 49 s 3
弓	bow, archery		KYŪ / yumi	r 57 s 3
弔	mourn, condole		CHŌ / tomura*u*	r 57 s 4
刀	sword	-	TŌ / katana	r 18 s 2
刃	blade	-	JIN / ha	r 18 s 3
及	attain	-	KYŪ / oyo*bu*..	r 29 s 3
了	finish; understand		RYŌ / #	r 6 s 2
子	child	-	SHI SU / ko	r 39 s 3
口	mouth	-	KŌ KU / kuchi	r 30 s 3
日	day; Japan; sun, Sunday		NICHI JITSU / hi -ka	r 72 s 4
目	eye; -th	#	MOKU BOKU / me ma-	r 109 s 5
且	moreover, besides	#	ka*tsu*	r 1 s 5
皿	dish	-	# / sara	r 108 s 5
母	mother	-	BO / haha	r 80 s 5
田	rice field	-	DEN / ta	r 102 s 5
甲	1st; shell		KŌ KAN / #	r 102 s 5
凸	convex	-	TOTSU / #	r 17 s 5
凹	concave, hollow		Ō / #	r 17 s 5
四	four	-	SHI / yo yo+ yo'+ yon	r 31 s 5
用	task; use, employ		YŌ / mochi*iru*	r 101 s 5
冊	books	-	SATSU SAKU / #	r 13 s 5
円	circle; *yen*		EN / maru*i*	r 13* s 4
丹	vermilion; sincerely		TAN / #	r 3 s 4
月	month; moon; Monday		GETSU GATSU / tsuki	r 74 s 4

1	33
2	34
3	35
4	36
5	37
6	38
7	39
8	40
9	41
10	42
11	43
12	44
13	45
14	46
15	47
16	48
17	49
18	50
19	51
20	52
21	53
22	54
23	55
24	56
25	57
26	58
27	59
28	60
29	61
30	62
31	**63**
32	64

千	斤	斥	丘	氏
thousand	*kin*	repel	hill	family name
-	-	-	-	
SEN	KIN	SEKI	KYŪ	SHI
chi	#	#	oka	uji
r 24 s 3	r 69 s 4	r 69 s 5	r 1 s 5	r 83 s 4
乏	升	我	毛	手
scarcity; poverty	*sho*; measure	I, my; self; selfish	hair, fur	hand
BŌ	SHŌ	GA	MŌ	SHU
tobo*shii*	masu	ware wa	ke	te ta
r 4 s 4	r 24 s 4	r 62 s 7	r 82 s 4	r 64 s 4
垂	乗	重		
droop	ride	heavy; layered		
-	-			
SUI	JŌ	JŪ CHŌ		
ta*reru..*	no*ru..*	omo*i* kasa+ -e		
r 32 s 8	r 4 s 9	r 166 s 9		
午	矢	年	缶	々
noon	arrow	year	tin can	ditto (see footnote)
-	-	-	-	#
GO	SHI	NEN	KAN	#
#	ya	toshi	#	r - s -
r 24 s 4	r 111 s 5	r 51 s 6	r 121 s 6	
勺	夕	久	匁	欠
shaku	evening	long time	*monme*	lack
	-	-	-	-
SHAKU	SEKI	KYŪ KU	#	KETSU
#	yu	hisa*shii*	monme	ka*ku..*
r 20 s 3	r 36 s 3	r 4 s 3	r 20 s 4	r 76 s 4

々 indicates duplication of the kanji it follows, and takes its reading from that kanji (sometimes the reading is slightly modified).

■   ...

..

入	八	心	必	父
enter; put in, let in	eight	heart	inevitable	father
NYŪ	- HACHI	- SHIN	- HITSU	- FU
hai*ru* i+	ya ya'+ ya+ yō	kokoro	kanara*zu*	chichi
r 11 s 2	r 12 s 2	r 61 s 4	r 61 s 5	r 88 s 4

升	我	飛	為	幽	○
sho; measure	I, my; self; selfish	fly, jump	do; purpose	deep; hidden; remote; ...	zero (see footnote)
SHŌ	GA	HI	I	YŪ	REI
masu	ware wa	to*bu*..	#	#	zero maru
r 24 s 4	r 62 s 7	r 183 s 9	r 86* s 9	r 52 s 9	r - s -

○ Is not officially a kanji but is used with Japanese numerals, for example in telephone numbers.

1	33
2	34
3	35
4	36
5	37
6	38
7	39
8	40
9	41
10	42
11	43
12	44
13	45
14	46
15	47
16	48
17	49
18	50
19	51
20	52
21	53
22	54
23	55
24	56
25	57
26	58
27	59
28	60
29	61
30	62
31	63
32	**64**

Table 1: Radicals

This table lists the traditional radicals: there are 214 in all, but some (omitted here) are not used among the *jōyō* kanji. The numbers in this table are the radical numbers used in the Fast Finder (and are fairly universally agreed). Some radicals are slightly distorted when appearing as parts of kanji; and you will see that some of the radicals have several different forms. Some older forms not used in the modern *jōyō* kanji have been omitted.

1	一		24	十	49	己	72	日		
2	丨		25	卜	50	巾	73	曰		
3	丶		26	卩 巳	51	干	74	月		
4	丿 亅		27	厂	52	幺	75	木		
5	乙 乚		28	厶	53	广	76	欠		
6	亅		29	又	54	廴	77	止		
7	二		30	口	55	廾	78	歹		
8	亠		31	囗	56	弋	79	殳		
9	人 亼 亻		32	土	57	弓	80	母 毋 毌		
10	儿		33	士	58	彐 彑	81	比		
11	入		34	夂	59	彡	82	毛		
12	丷 八 八		35	夊	60	彳	83	氏		
13	冂 冂		36	夕	61	心 忄 忄	84	气		
14	冖		37	大	62	戈	85	水 氺 氵		
15	冫		38	女	63	戸	86	火 灬		
16	几 几		39	子	64	手 扌	87	爪 爫		
17	凵		40	宀	65	支	88	父		
18	刀 刂		41	寸	66	攴 攵	90	爿		
19	力		42	小 ⺌ ⺍	67	文	91	片		
20	勹		44	尸	68	斗	92	牙		
21	匕		46	山	69	斤	93	牛		
22	匚		47	川 巛	70	方	94	犬 犭		
23	匸 匚		48	工	71	无	95	玄		

Table 1: Radicals (continued)

96	玉 王	124	羽	150	谷	180	音	
98	瓦	125	老 耂	151	豆	181	頁	
99	甘	126	而	152	豕	182	風	
100	生	127	耒	154	貝	183	飛	
101	用	128	耳	155	赤	184	食 飠	
102	田	129	聿 肀	156	走	185	首	
103	疋 疋	130	肉 月	157	足 ⻊	186	香	
104	疒	131	臣	158	身	187	馬	
105	癶	132	自	159	車	188	骨	
106	白	133	至	160	辛	189	高	
107	皮	134	臼	161	辰	190	髟	
108	皿	135	舌	162	辶	191	鬥	
109	目	136	舛	163	阝	193	鬲	
110	矛	137	舟	164	酉	194	鬼	
111	矢	138	艮 艮	165	釆	195	魚	
112	石	139	色	166	里	196	鳥	
113	示 礻	140	艹	167	金	198	鹿	
115	禾 穴	141	虍	168	長	199	麦	
116	穴 穴	142	虫	169	門	200	麻	
117	立	143	血	170	阝	201	黄	
118	竹 ⺮	144	行	172	隹	203	黒	
119	米	145	衣 衤	173	雨	207	鼓	
120	糸	146	西 襾	174	青	209	鼻	
121	缶	147	見	175	非	210	斉	
122	罒	148	角	176	面	211	歯	
123	羊 羊	149	言	177	革	212	龍 竜	

Table 2: Non-Traditional Radicals

The radical given in the Fast Finder is that used in the 'New Nelson' and 'Compact Nelson' kanji dictionaries[1]. In most cases this is the traditional historical radical. Where not, the radical number has an asterisk, and the kanji appears in the table below.

The table gives the traditional radical and for comparison (where differing from the traditional radical) the radical associated with the kanji in Halpern[2] and in 'Classic' editions (up to 1997) of Nelson. In many cases, the reason that these kanji are allocated a non-traditional radical is that in the course of the kanji being gradually modified and simplified down the centuries, the original radical has undergone (sometimes drastic) modification or has even disappeared entirely.

New Nel.		Trad.	Halp.	Classic Nel.
1	万	140	1	1
1	与	134	1	1
1	並	117	1	12
1	両	11	1	1
2	衰	145		2
6	予	152	6	6
6	争	87	6	4
9	体	188	9	9
9	全	11	9	9
9	会	73		9
9	舎	135	9	9
9	舗	135	9	9
10	党	203	10	42
13	内	11	13	2
13	円	31	13	13
14	写	40	14	14
16	処	141	16	34
22	区	23		22
22	匹	23		22
22	医	164	23	22
22	匿	23		22
24	単	30	42	3
27	厳	30	42	4
29	双	172	29	29
29	収	66	29	29

New Nel.		Trad.	Halp.	Classic Nel.
29	叙	66	29	29
30	台	133	30	28
30	号	141	30	30
30	営	86	42	30
32	声	128	33	32
32	売	154	33	32
32	壱	33		32
32	壮	33		32
32	塩	197	32	32
34	夏	35	35	1
34	変	149	34	8
41	寿	33	41	3
44	尽	108	44	44
49	巻	26	49	49
50	帰	77	18	58
56	弐	154		1
58	当	102	42	42
60	術	144		60
60	街	144		60
60	衝	144		60
60	衛	144		60
60	衡	144		60
67	斉	210		
67	斎	210		
72	旧	134	72	2

New Nel.		Trad.	Halp.	Classic Nel.
72	曲	73		72
72	更	73		72
72	最	73		72
72	曹	73		72
72	書	73		72
72	替	73		72
75	来	9	75	4
75	巣	47	42	3
77	歯	211		
86	為	87	86	3
86	点	203	86	25
109	冒	13	109	72
109	県	120	109	42
109	着	123		
117	竜	212		
130	服	74		130
130	朕	74		130
130	朗	74		130
130	期	74		130
130	朝	74		130
130	有	74		130
130	望	74		130
169	闘	191	169	169
181	頼	154		181

1   A.N. Nelson: the Modern Reader's Japanese-English Character Dictionary, Tuttle, Tokyo & Rutland, Vermont, revised edn. 1997; compact edn. abridged by J.H. Haig, 1999.
2   J. Halpern, New Japanese-English Character Dictionary, Kenkyusha, Tokyo, 1990.